WALTHER SPEAKS TO THE CHURCH

Selected Letters

WALTHER SPEAKS TO THE CHURCH

Selected Letters

C. F. W. WALTHER

Edited by Carl S. Meyer

Publishing House
St. Louis London

BX
8080
W3
A4131

Concordia Publishing House, St. Louis, Missouri
Concordia Publishing House Ltd., London, E. C. 1
© 1973 Concordia Publishing House
Library of Congress Catalog Card No. 72-94583
ISBN 0-570-03514-7
MANUFACTURED IN THE UNITED STATES OF AMERICA

To
Oliver R. Harms

CONTENTS

FOREWORD

C. F. W. Walther (1811 – 1887) is generally recognized as the outstanding Lutheran theologian in North America in the nineteenth century. He is the foremost theologian of The Lutheran Church – Missouri Synod. Theologian and churchman, he dominated the Synod during the first forty years of its existence. He served as president of the Synod for seventeen of those forty years (1847 – 50; 1864 – 78). He was the first professor of Concordia Seminary after it was transferred to St. Louis from Altenburg, Perry County, Missouri. He held that position for the remainder of his life, and in 1854 he was designated the president of the institution.

Walther's influence did not depend on the official posts he held. His leadership was recognized even before the formation of the Missouri Synod, for he emerged as the leader of the Saxon immigrants soon after their arrival in Missouri. He was largely responsible for exposing the aberrations of Martin Stephan, who had brought the group to Missouri. He reconciled the factions among the immigrants, overcoming the anticlericals in their midst by an emphasis on a concept of the church that reassured these exiles in a strange land. The Altenburg Debate (April 1841) was a turning point in the career of the young theologian, a few months before his thirtieth birthday. The importance of this colloquy cannot be overestimated, because immediately thereafter Walther took the place of his late brother, Hermann, as pastor of Trinity Lutheran Church in St. Louis. That post gave him a base of operation, a strategic location, and financial resources.

There, too, he developed into a pulpit orator and sermonizer of consummate skill. Not an inconsiderable portion of his leadership ability came from the high regard in which he was held as a preacher. He was a skilled dialectician, who could hold his own in theological discussions on every level. He seemed almost always to be prepared, ready to marshall arguments from the Scriptures, the Lutheran Confessions, and the Lutheran theologians of the sixteenth and seventeenth centuries. His speaking ability was matched by his well-stocked memory; apt quotations and erudite references gave substance to his extemporaneous remarks and his formal presentations.

Walther's pen was a fluent one. The contributions he made by way of the popular religious periodical he founded, *Der Lutheraner* (1844), were widely recognized. The technical theological journal, *Lehre und Wehre* (1855), of which, too, he was editor, assured him a hearing before the German-tongued theologians of this country. His books were recognized as solid contributions to the current theological output. They dealt with the topic of church and ministry, an issue of major proportions in the nineteenth century. His postils and sermon books were widely used in groups who could not have the services of a regular pastor every Sunday and had to rely on reading services *(Lesegottesdienste)*. His work on pastoral theology, although it relied heavily on a sixteenth-century prototype, gave practical guidance to men who for the most part knew only the dependence of the church on the territorial governments in their *Länder*.

Many of these men, pastors in a pluralistic society, often deficient in their theological education, turned to Walther for advice. A large number of them had sat at his feet between 1861 and 1875, while the "practical seminary" was located in St. Louis. These men, who far outnumbered the students in the "theoretical seminary," had no training in the languages (Greek and Hebrew, and often even Latin); they were not university graduates. To preach, to catechize, and to minister pastoral care were their tasks. Their vocational decisions usually came when they were young adults, beyond the adolescent years. Often these inner calls were tantamount to conversion experiences. These men came under the influence of Walther soon after that decision; his fierce confessionalism impinged itself indelibly on their hearts and minds.

Walther commanded deep loyalties. By the same token he could arouse lasting enmities. Men reverenced him as "a highly esteemed brother in Christ." Others regarded him as an autocrat, although the former greatly outnumbered the latter. Paradoxically he could be humble, winsome, deferential in his dealings with others; he could be haughty, proud, and at times even inconsiderate.

The range of his correspondence gives evidence of his great influence, the dependence of many pastors within the Synod on him, and his willingness to be of service. His letters have a constant refrain— "I am overwhelmed with work. . . . Please be satisfied with this little bit." Nevertheless, they were filled with practical advice and answers to a variety of questions. Not all his letters have survived by any means. Most of the letters addressed to him were destroyed, likely by Walther himself. Generally the letters he wrote are in his own hand, difficult to decipher. Sometimes he used copyists, but not too frequently. He was without a secretary during most of his life and found it difficult to use one.

The present collection of letters is meant to show the range of his concerns for the church. His concerns made his answers to questions definite and sure. He seldom admitted that he did not know the answers to the questions posed him. These letters are grouped about topics, and most often only an excerpt from a letter is given. This is not a critical edition of these letters.

As the reader studies these letters, made to various individuals at various times and under various circumstances, he will be struck with several consistent notes. The loudest is the evangelical approach Walther takes to the problems pastors pose to him and to the theological questions they ask of him. Walther's readiness to take the weaknesses of individuals into consideration, the allowances he made for ignorance and lack of understanding, the patience he counseled in difficult situations were bred and nurtured by the eminence he gave the Gospel. Walther was not a legalist. His repeated advice to his fellow pastors not to exercise lordship over their congregations was grounded solidly in his Gospel approach.

However, one cannot miss the note that called for doctrinal consistency with the Lutheran Symbols. Walther would not denigrate Scripture; to him it was the Word of God. Precious to him were also the Confessions of the Lutheran Church. Among them he valued the Augsburg Confession most highly. His theology was repristinated from the seventeenth-century theologians. This is evident also in his letters.

How much does Pietism crop up unwittingly in his letters? It is difficult to tell. One can detect traces of it, but it is not a dominant note. True, there is not an inconsiderable amount of emotionalism in his letters. Walther, however, grew up in the Age of Romanticism, and its roots in part were fed by Pietism. Sentiment had to be a part of his communications.

Because the letters are not given here in full, many personal references are missing. They show that Walther was acutely aware of the personal dimensions of his correspondents. So, too, greetings to wives and friends of the recipients are omitted. There are a considerable number of letters to his children: especially to Magdalene, wife of Pastor Stephan Keyl; to Julia, wife of Pastor Henry Niemann; and

11

to Ferdinand, his son. These letters contain family news, references to grandchildren, his wife, and mutual acquaintances. Only a few of these letters are given in excerpted form.

The letters reveal the man. Walther did not write these letters for publication; he was not an Erasmus. The conclusions of his letters often refer to the burdens he bore. Many of them are extremely personal. They reveal a sentimental aspect of Walther. We wish that we could have translated and reproduced more of them.

Only a few of these letters have previously been translated; most of them have not been published before. I have given such pertinent information about each letter in the Appendix.

Readers who may wish to learn more about C. F. W. Walther can be referred to the biography written by Dr. L. W. Spitz, *The Life of Dr. C. F. W. Walther* (St. Louis: Concordia Publishing House, 1961). The undersigned edited *Moving Frontiers: Readings in the History of The Lutheran Church—Missouri Synod* (St. Louis: Concordia Publishing House, 1964), a 500-page book, which contains an authoritative account of the Synod. He also edited an earlier volume of letters by C. F. W. Walther, *Letters of C. F. W. Walther: A Selection* (Philadelphia: Fortress Press, 1969). Only one letter from that collection is repeated in part in the present collection.

I am indebted to many for assistance and help in compiling this volume. The Rev. John Pohanka, as a graduate fellow in the School for Graduate Studies, has put me greatly in debt to him for his ready and effective cooperation. Dr. Robert Kolb, who previously served as a fellow on the "Walther project," likewise rendered valuable services. Mr. Michael Moore's services on this project must be acknowledged. Of great help were scores of pastors who willingly took on the labor of love of translating letters. We cannot enumerate them by name here, nor have we used the contributions of all of them. Their help is deeply appreciated. Walther is difficult to translate. Not all his letters are in polished shape. Paragraphing was added in the translations, and sentences in the original were broken up in the translations. The translators have caught the spirit of Walther as a writer of many letters. If they had been forced to wrestle with his handwriting, they might have despaired. The transcription of his letters by Prof. Werner Karl Wadewitz, subsidized by a grant from the Aid Association for Lutherans to Concordia Historical Institute, makes a volume such as this possible. Our gratitude goes out to him, to Concordia Historical Institute, and to the Aid Association for Lutherans. Walther had difficulty with using secretaries. I would be severely handicapped without them and herewith extend my thanks to them, especially to my wife, Lucille.

I have dedicated this volume to the Rev. Dr. Oliver R. Harms, past president of The Lutheran Church—Missouri Synod and director of its 125th anniversary committee. He is greatly responsible for encouraging the production of this volume in commemoration of the first president of the Synod. Most of all, however, this dedication is a recognition of Dr. Harms' churchmanship and his many services to the Missouri Synod.

If this volume of extracts from Walther's correspondence has a valid message to the church today, especially to The Lutheran Church—Missouri Synod, the cooperate efforts of students, pastors, secretaries, editors, and publisher will be satisfied.

6 June 1972

CARL S. MEYER

13

I. About Unity and Fellowship

Unity is a prominent theme in Walther's letters. He tells about the unity that existed among the Saxon immigrants before they organized a synod. He longed for unity with other like-minded Lutherans. Isolation, separatism, sectarianism, and dissension were obnoxious to him. The boast of orthodoxy was not enough to create unity where a lack of love was evident. The individual letters given here, however, generally link love and truth.

1. Walther's first letter to Dr. Wilhelm Sihler is a warm affirmation of the need for unity, either within a formal organization or outside a structure. He admitted that among the Saxon immigrants there was a fear of clerical dominance because of their experience with Martin Stephan. He mentions the fact that he began the publication of Der Lutheraner *(7 September 1844) "to call the orthodox Christians together."*

For a long time I have been sighing within myself because of the lone stance into which I was pressed, and often this has become almost unbearable for me. For, ah! how grave is the danger that detached congregations will only give birth to new sects! True, it is my conviction that in order to possess all the rights and treasures of the church, no congregation is so dependent on another that both must be under one uniform church government. But how dare we hope to be preserved in the fellowship of *one* faith, *one* mind, *and* one voice if we despise an external union with those who now share our same confession before the world when such union is possible?

Having previously yielded in utter delusion to the leadership of Stephan, we have special reason to search for orthodox brethren in order to join with them externally. Otherwise, we ourselves would give the enemies the right to regard and treat us as a special sect. And God knows that under Stephan we ourselves were minded to do nothing else than prove that we were perfectly loyal to the Lutheran Church. Nothing, however, has let us miss just this very thing more than our stubborn isolation. The more fatal and destructive this got to be for us the more we now yearn for the most painstaking preservation of the church's catholicity and for the avoidance of separatism in every form.

Welcome, therefore, dear brother! With great joy I extend to you my hand. I am doing this together with my colleague here, Pastor J. F. Bünger, who is my colaborer in this congregation. I am sorry that I am not able to inform you of the thinking of the other pastors here in the West who are united with us in faith. I shall, however, without delay send your kind letter and that of Pastor Ernst to the latter and urge them to express themselves.

. . . .

The fifth question: "With whom do the Saxon pastors form a synod? Are they alone for themselves?" — Between us pastors (namely, Löber, Keyl, Gruber in Perry County, Schieferdecker and Fürbringer in Illinois, Wege in Benton County, Mo., Brohm in New York, me and my colleague Bünger, and Pastor Geyer, who is just now entering on his ministry in Watertown, Wis. Terr.) there exists a oneness of faith and confession, agreement in our views on how to conduct the office of the ministry, the best possible conformity in regard to liturgy, and the like. In all this, we carry on a constant exchange of letters among us in which we share our experiences, and counsel, exhort, comfort, reprove, and encourage one another. Finally, our mutual relations are marked by a most intimate friendship. Also the congregations that have been formed by those who emigrated with us associate with one another in an active and brotherly fashion. However, though all this is true, a real ecclesiastical union has still not been effected.

Our chief objective so far was that we all become firmly grounded in the pure Lutheran doctrine. Our overriding aspiration was steadily to exchange our thoughts and convictions in conversation and by way of correspondence, and in this manner jointly to work our way out of the Stephan errors and toward the pure truth. By the disclosure of the Stephanite deception we were driven into the writings of Luther. These, besides God's Word, all of us have studied, almost exclusively, and we believe that under the Spirit's guidance we have now become properly enlightened through this matchless bequest. We had grown to be distrustful of all our judgments; everything was, therefore, subjected anew to the strictest scrutiny. A thorough reformation in doctrine and practice — that was, up to now, the goal toward which we thought we had to strive first.

In this we, however, by no means want to abandon ourselves to a false spiritual course. We clearly realize that without an external union of the orthodox Lutheran clerics and their congregations the unity of the Spirit and thus the purity in doctrine cannot be preserved, and much less will the talents of the individual be put to use for the common good. My answer to your question therefore is: We are working toward the establishment of a uniform church government.

The sixth question: "Would it be possible for you to enter into complete union with our brethren?" — I consider this not only to be possible but also extremely desirable and very, very promising for the spiritual welfare of us all. Yes, I consider that to be inescapable for conscience' sake, if union is at all possible.

However, I must remark that in the entire West there are German demagogs galore who do their utmost to make any sort of synodical union detestable. Even well-meaning people do not remain entirely unaffected. Consequently, a certain fear of organizations such as this is prevalent here. They dread clerical rule. In addition, our emigrant congregations especially are rather apprehensive of everything that in the slightest degree is reminiscent of hierarchism, since they suffered so terribly under the tyranny of Stephan. Therefore it should first be discussed how this very desirable ecclesiastical union could be initiated without arousing the suspicion that the shepherds are contemplating to rule over the flocks or that the establishment could, at least, easily lead to this.

I for my own part am ready for whatever possible sacrifice that would be required in order to bring about a church union. For that very reason I also (though greatly lacking the necessary gifts for this) in God's name still ventured to send such a small paper as *Der Lutheraner* out into the world and to offer it to the church of God in America so that, at least I for my part, insignificant though it be, would do all I can to call the orthodox Christians together.

2. While Walther was on a visit in Europe in 1860 to regain his health, he wrote a letter in which he described the unity he perceived within the Missouri Synod. Agreement in doctrine, mutual confidence, a readiness to discuss differences in order to remove them, and a longing to unite with others are characteristics of the unity within the Synod. The members of the Synod are ready to learn from the former teachers of the church, such as Luther. To Walther unity was a precious gift.

An entirely different kind [of unity], in contrast, is that in which our Synod stands. Pupils of the same teachers, of a Luther and his

17

faithful followers, we have come to the clear knowledge and living conviction that our dear Evangelical Lutheran Church, as she has set forth her doctrine in her Confessions, agreeing in all points with the Word of God, is the continuation of the old, apostolic church; in short, at the present time the only orthodox church. United under this great principle we are knit together by a cordial, fraternal confidence. We are, in spite of all the jealous concern for our unity in doctrine and faith, free, nevertheless, from every inquisitorial spirit, which can so easily convert the fraternal bond into oppressive iron shackles. So, too, mutual confidence prevents us from disregarding those differences in doctrine which become evident and are at hand, to cover them up and to submerge them. Instead of declaring such points "open questions" and entering into mutual compromises in order to remain outwardly united, we bring them out in the open as manifest differences. We do not desist from seeking and searching in the Word of God and in the testimonies of the church and the teachers of the church, by colloquies and disputations privately and publicly, until unity has been attained also in those points in which it might have suffered loss. . . .

We subscribe wholeheartedly to the well-known maxim *In necessariis unitas, in dubiis libertas, in omnibus caritas* (in essentials, unity; in doubtful things, liberty; in all things, charity). We do so, however, not in a unionistic sense, which places even the doctrine of the means of grace into the category of doubtful things. We do so in this sense: that we gladly permit anyone to harbor his private opinions in matters which are not contrary to the Word of God, as long as he does not attempt to subject anyone else's conscience to his.

So little is unity in the form and method of doctrine the goal of our endeavors that we rather heartily rejoice in the multiplicity of spiritual gifts, which in this respect are given free play for their development.

Our union stipulates agreement in ceremonies only insofar as this unity is required by the confessional rites of our church. Unity in practice is of great value to us, to be sure, but only insofar as the unhindered edification of the church depends upon a common foundation and as faithfulness to the Confessions requires it.

Strongly united as we are now among ourselves, our unity is not, however, a sectarian one. On the contrary, an inner longing for unity with all other denominations enlivens and inspires us. The less this unity among us is cold and abstract, but rather a unity of the spirit in the bond of peace, a unity of sentiments and cordial love, so much the more it urges us to pursue unity with all Christians, especially with those who carry before them the same confessional banner. We have already exercised so much effort in that direction, by the grace and impetus of God, that because of this we must bear the insult of hearing the accusation from false brethren that we harbor in our bosom "an eagerness for conquest."

. . . .

Oh, how I rejoice, therefore, that God has given me the great grace to participate in the fellowship of our Synod! To the praise of the Lord I acknowledge that I perceive in her a return of the days of our fathers' unity of faith. May the gracious and merciful God, from whom this unity is a pure gift of grace, continue to preserve it among us. May He make us faithful that also on our part we may preserve this precious jewel. As He has established a deep-felt unity between us and our fathers, already resting in their graves, may He unite us to an ever greater degree with our brethren living near us and battling at our side. May He make us constantly stronger and more faithful through our unity. May He — and this is my final wish today — help me that renewed in strength I may soon return to the circle of my brethren and that I may continue to enjoy the blessing which I have enjoyed within it up to this time until the day of my death, when I hope to enter through Christ into the blessed fellowship of the Church Triumphant. Amen.

3. Walther advises a member of the Breslau Synod in Germany not to withdraw from that synod, even though errors persisted in the congregation. He did not wish to do anything contrary to God's command or contrary to love. The letter exemplifies Walther's concern that love be exercised in one's relations with fellow believers.

We fully recognize that if no change for the better appears, you cannot in good conscience join with the party of the Supreme Ecclesiastical Board in Breslau nor with Pastor Diedrich as members of one of his congregations if you want to remain true Lutherans. Nevertheless, we are united in the conviction, based on God's Word, that you cannot break away from your present communion until it has been proven that it has been impenitent in its error. What great and abominable errors prevailed, e. g., in the Galatian congregations or churches! Yet, not only does the apostle continue to call them congregations or churches, and their members his dear brethren, but he also does not demand of the few who without doubt had remained in the truth in these congregations that they break away from their corrupted congregations. He tried first of all to lead the congregations back to the truth from which they had broken away. So we think, dear brother, that this is what you must do, too, in Prussia.

You dare not break away from your present communion until you have exhausted every means at your command to convince them of their error and to restore them, without result, or until they have run you out as disturbers of the peace, rabble-rousers, and the like because of your witness for the truth against error. I suppose you will say that whatever you yourself could do personally you have already done, and that it was all without result. If so, I must still tell you that in spite of this the time has not yet come when we Missourians can, on the basis of your request to us, embrace you in such a way that we would send you a pastor without further effort on your part. From our point of view you must necessarily have exhausted every means to lead your present communion to the truth—and thereby yourselves back to it also—and gotten no result before we could send you a pastor, or we would be making ourselves guilty of the sin of schism.

4. In a letter to Sihler Walther wrote at some length about personalities among Lutheran leaders in Germany who were about to organize the Lutheran Free Church. Complete unanimity cannot be hoped for within a synod. In this same letter he wrote at length about some pastors who left the Leipzig Mission in India. That portion of the letter is not reproduced here. The letter concludes: "It is evident that God wants to bring those together more and more who with us wish to cling fast to the doctrine of the Reformation. God give us wisdom, humility, and constancy!"

No, my d[ear] Sihler, that is neither a Christian nor a Lutheran spirit. That is the spirit of a man who, so to speak, was born to be a sectarian leader. Had such a spirit prevailed among us originally, there would be no Missouri Synod. What differences arose during the first decade of our synodical history! Entirely different and more important than between R[uhland] and H[oerger]. If we had behaved towards each other as H[oerger] does to R[uhland], everything would have exploded in short order, like ignited powder. May God preserve our communion from the inroad of such a spirit. This is not the spirit that seeks only the glory of God and the welfare of souls, but the fanaticism of unacknowledged ambition. I myself have suffered too bitterly from such a spirit, and my soul is not yet healed fully from its wounds that I will permit myself to be trapped by it once more, nor will I submit to it. Even the purest confession according to the letter cannot trap me. In their day Stephan and Grabau were relatively more orthodox than everybody else. But we know what those suffered who submitted to their dictation for that reason and thought that no false spirit could therefore rule with such a confession; and for the same reason one put the best construction on everything that caused misgiving, that chafed one, or one swallowed it.

I would rather have spoken with you first, but I regarded it dangerous to delay, and for that reason I have already shared these, my present convictions, with R[uhland]. I also said that I thought it best if those who had confidence in one another would, in God's name, unite in a small synod. On the other hand, they should not invite H[oerger] and Wagner, who is now siding with H[oerger] but who will not last long under H[oerger]'s rod. They should no longer disturb them [Hoerger and Wagner] in their independent sympathies until eventually they also see that the ghosts they believe they now see are not from without but only in their own minds, and they themselves ask for admission.

If the brethren in Germany wait until finally they are all completely agreed without exception, then nothing will ever become of an orthodox synod. . . . But if they wish to force the organizing of a synod explicitly by all, H[oerger] and W[agner] included (while one does not trust the other and H[oerger] and W[agner] continuously regard it with Argus eyes, wondering whether the "American-Missourian papacy" will not attempt to bind their consciences, rule over them, impose distasteful usages and arrangements on them, etc.), they would be building the synod on a mine, which would threaten to explode any minute, or founding a robber synod. However, those who have acknowledged each other as brethren in the faith ought not postpone the matter because of a few stubborn heads, else it will be jeopardized entirely.

From the time he was in the Breslau Synod and later through correspondence with the Immanuel Synod Wagner is filled with dreadful obsessions of slavery — in which the preachers here in our Synod ostensibly linger. Even when his scruples are satisfied again and again, they pop up again and again. Then (what astonishes me greatly) he denies that he was ever satisfied, even if previously he expressly gave the assurance that he was. Of course, I don't despair of such a character, but I think it is the greatest foolishness to include someone like that in a synod that is just being organized. First give him a chance to look at it from the outside; let him investigate if anything else rules in our Synod but the Word of God and, as far as subjection is concerned, if this is required only from this or that one and not from everyone. To be sure, anyone who does not want to subject himself to God's Word had better not venture into our midst; there he would not find a peaceful hour. However, someone who wishes that [subjection to God's Word] is the freest man on earth among us.

Don't be taken in by the talk H[oerger] and W[agner] carry on, that R[uhland] is not a "genuine" representative of Missouri. This kind of talk is evidently politics, since W[agner] was full of misgivings from the start not only about R[uhland] but also about our Synod and full of anxiety about its decrees (a contributing factor to that may be that W[agner] practices usury and therefore is afraid that he will develop an uneasy conscience among us). I know from H[oerger]'s letters to Krauss that H[oerger] also is full of misgivings about the freedom of the pastors in our Synod and about the preference our synodical members have for our Synod ahead of every other communion.

5. *Reconciliation is necessary for anyone who is at odds with others within the Synod, if he wants to return to service in the Synod, Walther writes.*

As far as I know, not only are you still unreconciled with Dr. Sihler and Prof. Fleischmann, but you continue to maintain very serious charges against the former. Your return to the service of the church within our Synod, which we could all certainly welcome with greatest joy, cannot possibly take place until you have taken the necessary steps toward reconciliation with these gentlemen. You know that the members of our Synod are united as brothers in the truth; this relationship would be broken in fact, if some members would want to ignore a rupture in the brotherly relationship between others. Therefore, I beg you, submit yourself, as is fitting for a Christian, and try to bring about a reconciliation between yourself and them in a Christian way. Unless it can be decided on which side the only or the greatest wrong lies, I can give you no other advice on the basis of God's Word, especially if you do not intend to return to our Synod. May God guide your heart to do what is pleasing to the Lord.

6. *Unity must have its basis in a love for truth. This brings blessings.*

About the synodical address, since you want to hear my ideas about it, I would say that everywhere a desire for unity is stirring; that, however, it can be God-pleasing and can accomplish its goals only if it does not arise from trust in numbers, organization, external peace, and the like, but rather from love of the truth, for God's honor, for the soul's salvation. With that, one could refer to the earlier Henoticers, the Interim, the Helmstädt Synecretism, and the Prussian Union—all of them, resting on an evil basis, have only effected harm. On the other hand, Athanasius, Luther, Chemnitz, and others, for example, who despised every unity of persons without a unity in the truth, have accomplished not only great blessings but great unity.

7. *Truth is more important than peace. Love is not a mark of the church.*

Would Zech. 8:19 be a good text for your speech: "Love, Truth, and Peace"? With that [text] one could demonstrate how foolish it would be to seek peace first and then truth. Mentioning the passage from Luther's Commentary on Ps. 110:2 . . . and several [passages] from Luther's misgivings about Chancellor Bruck in 1541 . . . could serve well. – Or do you want to show that according to Christ's expression "by this all men will know that you are My disciples, if you have love for one another" (John 13:35), love still is not a *nota ecclesiae?* This would be rather difficult but very interesting and timely, since this area is now beclouded.

8. *Unity of doctrine is the greatest asset of the Missouri Synod, Walther writes. This unity is grounded in fidelity to the Lutheran Confessions.*

Our treasure is not our *size* but rather our *unity in doctrine* and that both in pastoral as well as in eccelesiastical practice. Should our Synod lose this treasure, then it will be ruined, and it will be devoured by the present American Lutheran bodies. We must not hide the fact that our present ministerial generation is not of the same calibre as that of our Synod's first decade. The easier it is to establish congregations, the less easy it is to find men who had matured to the demands of self-denial, which nevertheless must be made of our ministerium if it is to have genuine success. As great as the cry for preachers is everywhere, so great are the difficulties as a rule, after a call has been heeded, that the people really become obedient to God's Word. They do not want to fall back into paganism, but they are startled when they see, after the arrival of an orthodox preacher, what he understands by Christian congregational conduct. To this must be added that whenever an orthodox preacher begins his work, immediately the sectarians appear like robber bees to steal the honey which has been gathered with much hard work, with sighs and tears. . . .

23

9. Walther tells Pastor Brunn in Steeden, who was sending men to study at Concordia Theological Seminary for service in the Missouri Synod, that these men are of one mind and heart with their fellows.

From nowhere else than from you do we receive people who feel themselves so much at home here, who are so entirely of our spirit, and team up so readily with us. The spirit of innocence, faithfulness in doctrine, the spirit of self-denial, which does not seek its own advantage in life, together with the spirit of sensibleness in practice, which God has given us and your spiritual sons, which we have in common, have fused us so rapidly.

10. What is a Lutheran? He is one who does not separate from an orthodox church in which there are differences. In accord with the Augsburg Confession he is irenic and conservative.

I can only say Yea and Amen to what you have written about your relationship and public behavior toward the *Landeskirchen*. Even if our hot-blooded young Erlangen friends continue to think it goes too slowly, that cannot confuse us. A Lutheran is, so to say, conservative by nature and can be moved to break with the conditions in which God has placed him only if one forces him to act against his conscience. There is a great difference between an originally false churchly fellowship and an originally orthodox but degenerate [fellowship]. Above all, the empty permitting to exist of the correct faith does not make a fellowship orthodox. Only the behavior of those who are in it determines that. One must leave a heretical or schismatic fellowship, without consulting flesh and blood, or even a syncretistically constituted sect. This is not the case with a church that originally was orthodox but in which now untruth and heresy cause struggles. One abandons a sinking ship, not a leaky [one]. There is probably no better sublime evidence of the truly irenic and conservative sense of Lutheranism than the Augustana, to which indeed an ultimatum such as that of the Smalcald Articles had to be issued.

11. Walther's letter to Pastor Wilhelm Loehe in Neuendettelsau after his return in 1852 (he and Wyneken visited with Loehe) speaks of the accord reached by these churchmen. Walther's intense desire for unity is evident, as is his loyalty to the Lutheran Confessions. His readiness to cooperate with Loehe is seen in his agreement with Loehe about the teacher training institution in Michigan. "To walk hand in hand" with Loehe is his wish. He expresses his appreciation for the money being raised in Germany to build the second wing of the seminary in St. Louis. Loehe's "great love" gives Walther reason to believe that his apology will be accepted. In reading this letter we cannot escape the question, Why the break between Walther and Loehe? This letter does not answer the question. However, it is a testimony of Walther's high regard for Loehe.

First of all, please accept again our most cordial thanks for all the love and care you extended to us during our stay with you. God Himself must and surely will provide the best thanks by means of the blessing He will bestow on the peacemaking efforts that hold so much promise.

We arrived here safely on 2 February. The report about the outcome of our trip, namely the accord reached with you, esteemed pastor, was hailed with great joy everywhere. The numberless prayers offered by honest Christians have undoubtedly received the assurance that they have been heard. Also from others, such as the Ohio Synod, we received unsolicited testimony to the salutary impression elicited by the news that you did not sever relations with us but fashioned even firmer ties. It is therefore my hope that the last battle we fought with this and similar American synods, which desire to be Confessional, will indeed be the last one. After the close of our next synodical convention Wyneken and I plan to travel to Columbus, not to pave the way for an external union but for one that finds expression through spiritual and fraternal dialog. The situation with these people is very much different from that of many half-Lutherans in Germany. Many of these people are not the sort that have been content to sit idly by because of carnal considerations, but they have not yet made progress simply because the day has just begun to dawn for them.

When we arrived, we found the Grabau faction engaged in an extremely spiteful battle against us, and, seemingly, the reports concerning the outcome of our mission have irritated them even more. They have almost exclusively taken the line of demonstrating to us that the people who separated from them and whom we received were nothing but infamous people of whom we should only be ashamed and whose reception on our part has given the best evidence of the ungodliness of our principles. Oh, if we only knew of a way to peace which we could walk without violating our conscience, how happily we would walk it! However, as long as the peace negotiations are all to be opened with admissions of guilt only by us, we cannot take the initiative. We have received into membership only those of whom we were thoroughly convinced that they had been excommunicated by our opponents contrary to God's Word, or those who would be served with the means of grace only on the condition that they would repudiate us and agree to principles which we regard as wrong. Many of those whom we had to rebuke earlier because of their unfaithfulness to the Lutheran Confession are now joining the Grabau party. Instead of having to confess to us their former error, it now pleases them to be able to take revenge against us by joining in the anathemas hurled against us.

Now to the matter about which you had the kindness to write me. Pertaining to the disposition you made about the teachers seminary that is to be established, I must indeed confess that I was initially somewhat dejected when I heard the news about it; but only because of our dear Schaller, who was not only himself highly elated but whose entire congregation had likewise already enthusiastically adopted the idea of daring hopefully to see a proper institution blossom in their midst and under their care in the near future. However, these human, though not profane, considerations soon gave way to more appropriate ones about which you had the goodness to inform me. Therefore I now cheerfully resign myself to the change our plan has experienced, all the more since the rest of your most recent tidings open the prospect that our more northern colonies in Michigan will be expanded into a second Pennsylvania without the danger of gradually experiencing the formation of a similar German spirit and of Lutheranism. With a sincere heart I confess to you that I now have a completely different attitude than formerly over against Michigan and the great work developing there; I am thrilled by the hope that can no longer be diminished that American Germanism and Lutheranism will there finally receive a buttress and a fountain in which they may and also elsewhere will constantly refresh themselves.

. . . All in all, from now on it will be the Synod's sacred as well as precious obligation to walk hand in hand with you and the friends allied with you wherever it is feasible and to regard their general concerns as one body, of which they are not capable without you.

. . . .

Esteemed pastor, you will have found some items in the *Lutheraner* during our absence from here that may have offended you. Much to my astonishment and completely against my wishes this material from a private letter sent to St. Louis got into the periodical. I trust that because of your great love you will be able to forget this too, as with so many other things from the past.

II. About a Congregation's Relationship to the Synod

Several letters show Walther's view about the role of a synod over against a pastor and a congregation. The synod must be of help to congregations to safeguard the teaching in its midst. A pastor who belongs to the synod must abide by its constitution. However, Christian liberty permits a congregation the right to choose the synod, if it is an orthodox one, to which it wants to belong.

In case of a protest by a congregation, Walther as synodical president was careful to follow the proper procedures. He will not interfere, even as president of the Synod, until procedurally he is permitted to do so.

The jurisdiction of a congregation in admitting and excluding members Walther upholds rather decisively.

12. Even when pointing out procedures Walther stressed the desirability of peace in a congregation. This letter shows how careful Walther was to detail the proper procedures when members had a grievance against their pastor. Walther's repeated use of the term **Seelsorger** *in this letter likely was intended as a reminder of the basic relationship that existed between the members of the congregation and their pastor.*

You asked me whether it would be advisable and permissible that you would take Holy Communion from Pastor Moll because you have lost confidence in your pastor as your spiritual guardian and wish to separate yourselves from his care of souls but not from your congregation.

To this I answer as follows:

First, I beseech you earnestly not to regard these lines as proof that I wish to decide your question in any fashion or to judge you or your pastor *(Seelsorger)* right or wrong. Since I have not had the opportunity to hear both sides, I must withhold judgment about this. However, pertaining to the second [point] in your petition, you

27

cannot accept another pastor as long as it has not been proved that you are in the right and your pastor is in the wrong, and the latter will not put away his wrong.

Since, as you write, your congregation will not join in inviting the president of your District to investigate the cause of the current quarrel, the president surely cannot impose himself [on you]; according to the constitution of our Synod he simply is not allowed to do this. Now, if you believe that your pastor has committed a wrong that robs you of your confidence in him and that he persists in it, nothing remains for you but to accuse him before your president, whereupon the president or vice-president must investigate the basis for, or the lack of a basis for, your accusation, because a congregation may refuse to undergo an investigation but a pastor may not. With this I am in no wise urging you to accuse your pastor, because I simply cannot know whether you are in the right; but I am pointing out to you how it must be done in our Synod when members of a congregation experience a wrong from their pastor and cannot obtain a hearing either from him or from the congregation.

This matter disturbs me most deeply, and I wish from the bottom of my heart and entreat God that these circumstances that have broken into your congregation may be allayed, since they threaten to result in great spiritual harm, and that peace may again be restored.

13. In a sharply worded letter Walther tells an otherwise unknown layman that he as synodical president cannot step into the affairs of a local congregation. If he had the duty, threats would not be necessary.

According to your valued letter of the 14th of this month you are turning to me as the last court of appeal. You wish me to give an official decision in your affair with Trinity Congregation in Milwaukee. However, I must inform you that as synodical president I can do nothing in your matter because our synodical constitution lists only the following as the duties of the synodical president: "The synodical president etc. as such." (See Constitution, C. VI. C. par. 1.)

From that you can see that I do not have supervision over individual congregations or their pastors. Therefore when difficulties arise in individual congregations, I can intervene only when they voluntarily request my intervention and, moreover, only when both of the quarreling parties request it.

If it were my duty to deal with your matter officially, it would not have been necessary, as it were, to force me to meet my obligation, as you seem to want to do, first by threatening me with the loss of my "soul's salvation" and with my "accountability before the eternal Judge of the world."

14. Walther as president of the Synod would not interfere in a matter that belonged to a District. However, if his services were needed or desired, he would step in.

I have received a letter from Lochner dated the 10th of this month in which he reports to me that his congregation has voted to ask you and me if we would, after all, examine the _____ affair immediately. Naturally, I can do nothing in the matter as long as it is still before the District except to give assistance whenever and wherever it is wanted. Hence I have waited for your request. In case you want to know if I am ready to participate in an examination before the convention of the Northern District meets, I declare myself heartily willing. I certainly believe that the matter in Milwaukee is so serious that it urgently requires a prompt remedy. I will, therefore, if God gives me life and health, arrive in Milwaukee on the day that you set for the meeting of the participants in this matter.

15. In procedural matters between a congregation and the Synod Walther tried to be very scrupulous in his dealings. His advice to a pastor shows his desire for fairness, for maintaining the good reputation of the Synod, and for avoiding separatism.

Enclosed you will find the report you sent me. I am sending it back to you again after I have read it with my colleagues. I believe that since the matter has gone so far, the Synod must intervene now, if it does not wish to bear the blame because one of its ministers and one of its congregations has seriously gone astray on the wrong path. In fact I believe that you, whom one must consider as a partisan, ought to do nothing as a Visitor. Otherwise someone would say that you are both a partner and a judge as well. Therefore, the affair should immediately be given over to the District president, Pastor [Ottomar] Fuerbringer. Then it would be up to his conscience to decide in what way he believes he must intervene.

So that you are not compelled to work out a report again, I am sending you what you furnished me. In any case Pastor Fuerbringer should be given an insight into that which I have already voiced privately on request as my decision. It cannot be regarded as an official one, because it was based on the report of one party; however, it should be taken into consideration as a link in the chain of events in his consideration.

Now as far as those protesting are concerned, as I see it, you should not serve them as pastor until the matter is examined by the president and brought to a decision. You must not act here according to your own personal conviction, because every pastoral act affects our synodical relationship with Pastor _____ and his congregation, whose decision you cannot anticipate. Those protesting must also show through self-suffering that they are Christians who love Christian order and that they are willing to tolerate something for a while, rather than be guilty of a dangerous and pernicious separation.

16. Answering a series of questions from a woman, not otherwise identified, Walther says that membership in a synod is a human arrangement. A synod does not have the right to excommunicate a person; excommunication is the function of the local congregation.

Your third question was: can, etc.

I answer: No; since synodical association is not commanded by God but is a human arrangement and since each layman is free to associate with any orthodox congregation, there can be no sin against God's command deserving excommunication here; still much less if within the synod one person exercises power in such a way as to burden consciences.

Your fourth question was: can, etc.

I answer: According to God's Word the exclusion can be executed only by a congregation (that is, pastors and members) in which the one who is to be excommunicated is a member, for the apostle, when he wanted the man who had committed incest excommunicated, taught that this was to be done by the assembled congregation at Corinth, where the one who had committed incest was, 1 Corinthians 5:3-5, so the apostle gave the general rule, *"You yourselves, drive out the wicked person from among you"* 1 Corinthians 5:13. Those who are familiar with the language know that here is indicated that excommunication can be executed only by those in whose own midst the one to be excommunicated is found.

. . . .

Your sixth question was: can, etc.

I take the liberty concerning the first part of this question to direct you back to the reply to your third question. . . . It is absurd to want to do this to one who is already outside the synodical affiliation and to regard a person as godless because of this . . . as an amputated member of the Body of Christ and to make this declaration because she left an association that is just a human institution; thus, a person goes against Matthew 15:9 when he makes keeping human commandments the service of God and the failure to keep them a mortal sin.

17. A congregation can change its synodical affiliation, Walther writes. He kept the principle of Christian liberty in mind in making his decision.

. . . Because a synodical association is only a human order, there is no doubt that a congregation that is without a minister can select a minister from another synodical association and accordingly change to the association to which he belongs. So I would not think twice about admitting into our Synod a congregation that previously had belonged to the Canada Synod but no longer is able to have confidence in this [synod], all the more since the above named synod is trying to chain the congregation to itself by manipulating the deeds [for its property]. Briefly the choice of a synod is a matter of freedom.

Just as it is wrong when a synod chases after the congregation of another [synod], trying to draw it to itself without a call, so also it is self-evident that one accepts a congregation against which there is nothing in the way, if it wants to be admitted. Then it has only to notify the synod to which it formerly belonged that it is leaving. If the synod will not permit this, then it must be told that that is a major reason why one must leave it, because it [the synod] wants to bind the congregation to itself and thereby robs it [the congregation] of its freedom.

18. Walther advised Schwan how to deal with a pastor who did not wish to conform to the regulations of the Synod. The context of this extract shows that the recalcitrant was not open to corrections.

Why would there be the Synod, why the Visitors, if we do not help a congregation that has such a nuisance who robs it of all the joy of its ministry and with that of its intended blessing? It should not make you timid that he did not come to you; you must deal with him all the more seriously. Drive home with God's Word to explain directly that in this way he will be lost and that the blood of the souls he alienated from himself will be demanded of him. If he does not wish to belong to a synod that calls him to account, well, let him stand alone. He himself may answer before God that in this adiaphoron he insists on his freedom. We do not hold him, but as long as he is with us and wants to belong to our free union, he must submit himself to the constitution.

19. *To be admitted as members of a Missouri Synod congregation, it is not necessary, Walther writes, to recognize the proceedings of the Synod.*

According to the synodical constitution our congregation at Altenburg has full freedom and jurisdiction to receive those members who left it but want to return under certain conditions that preserve its confessional stance. I do not doubt that the above-mentioned congregation will receive those who return with open arms, if they only acknowledge their agreement with the faith of the congregation and confess that their separation was wrong. They may return even if "they think that they are bound by conscience to reunite only under protest against the proceedings begun by the Missouri Synod against Pastor Schieferdecker." At least I cannot personally view the recognition of the proceedings of the synod to which a congregation belongs as an absolutely necessary prerequisite for reception into a congregation.

20. *In a letter addressed to all pastors and congregations of the Missouri Synod, Walther, as president of the Synod, appeals for a special collection for the building needs of the Synod. He also pointed to the necessity for regular contributions for current expenses in a portion omitted here. Throughout, Walther's evangelical approach is evident.*

The precious congregations of our Synod everywhere, on both sides of the ocean, have the reputation that the Word they preach of the great love that God has for us has made them rich in diverse works of reciprocal love. And this is really so; be it said to God's honor that extensive lists of receipts in every issue of our *Lutheraner* openly testify to that. By the grace of God our precious congregations have become a sweet savor of Christ to many — among both those who are blessed and those who are lost.

It gives me a joyfulness to turn to your generous love with a heartfelt petition.

As you know, we are molding a Lutheran synod. This is not a union of pastors who now and then meet with several congregational members in order to legislate laws for the congregations, as the German Consistorium does. No, a synod such as ours is a union of congregations with united strength, existing almost as one man, for the purpose of providing first that our existing congregations are furnished with faithful teachers in church and school, and furthermore that our widely scattered fellow believers are gathered in congregations and also furnished with God's Word. All maintain the unity of the Spirit through the bond of peace, and thus the kingdom of God is built and extended farther and farther.

Actually our congregations should assemble together—every member—in order to hold a synodical convention. Since that is not possible, each congregation sends two persons as its representatives, a pastor and a lay delegate. The actual representatives at the synodical convention are not, therefore, a kind of ecclesiastical authority over congregations, rather nothing else but servants of the congregations who do only the necessary work, specifically that which is necessary for the entire union of congregations, and then they only advise. They do formulate resolutions, however, not to impose them on congregations as laws but rather only to suggest these to the congregations, who then have the right to examine them, and they [congregations] have the full freedom to either accept them or reject them.

When our representatives met in Fort Wayne last October, they were convinced, as you know, that if the existing institutions of our Synod should not decline, instead of moving forward, then we will have to build in Addison, Fort Wayne, and Springfield. Therefore they passed the resolution that the necessary new buildings be constructed in the above-mentioned places. So it is up to you, your precious congregations, either to approve and carry out this resolution or to reject it and leave it undone.

What will happen now, [my] dear brothers?—God has over-abundantly blessed our Synod. All our institutions for educating and training capable pastors and teachers, without which no church can exist for any length of time, are overcrowded. Therefore, it is necessary to provide more room. Should we now, so that if we do not have to build, tell the young people who want to devote themselves to the service of the church to go back home? Impossible! By God's grace our Synod has acquired a good reputation. From all sides we are fervently requested, "Come over here and help us! Oh, send us pastors and teachers!" God has deemed us worthy to be His instrument for building up the true Evangelical Lutheran Church in America, while it is in danger of perishing in our old homeland. Therefore, dare I not have the high hope that you, dear brothers, are ready and willing to do something about carrying out the great and blessed work that God has placed into our hands in this our new fatherland? I have no doubt about it.

So my first request is: Quickly select—haste is here necessary—one or more members of your congregation who are zealous for God's kingdom, and commission them to go from house to house and to collect contributions for the construction of the necessary new buildings mentioned. If each gives according to his ability with a willing heart out of thankfulness for the precious Word of God, which God has already given to him, then, in this way, as much as is needed will certainly be collected. Whoever cannot or does not wish to give the total amount that he wants to donate — let him set the day when he wishes to give the balance. When you have collected a small sum, then send it to your District treasurer and inform him, if you can, at what date and how much he can still expect [from you] later.

However, remember that this is not the pastor's business but your own business; it concerns a Christian opportunity for which we pastors, as your fellow Christians, will do our part. Our buildings are not pastors' buildings, and the synodical possessions of houses and property are not the possessions of the pastors, but rather your buildings, your possessions, and indeed, therefore, each member of your congregations also has a share in their ownership [lit., the right of a joint proprietor].

Oh, you precious congregations, do not lose the reputation that you have a faith that is active in love, and God will not leave you poorer because of your giving. Rather, He will bless you all the more in material things, for godliness has the promise of this and of the future life.

III. About the Church in Conflict

Walther defines the church as "a communion of the regenerate and renewed who are gathered in the Spirit." He will have nothing of the concept that the Lutheran Church is the one true church. He cites Luther and the Confessions to support his view.

Faithfulness to the Scriptures may mean controversies. Controversies are to be expected. However, even in translations the Scriptures can be believed.

Among the conflicts Walther faced was the Predestinarian Controversy.

21. What is the church? It can be defined only by the Scriptures. The Augsburg Confession gives the Scriptural exposition of the essence of the church. To be truly Lutheran it is necessary to go back to Luther's writings. The Lutheran church is not anxious to amass power.

You say that from now on you want to practice your whole Christianity and to exercise resolutely your position in, and in relation to, the church, whatever the cost may be. Who shall not rejoice at this? The angels in heaven rejoice over one sinner who repents; how much more do we fellow sinners have reason to rejoice when one who is also a sinner, who is also redeemed, who is also a brother, who has already laid hold on the Lord, resolves to serve Him with renewed, heightened, most genuine, and most reckless faithfulness.

You say, from now on the Word and only the Word shall make decisions for you and effect what it may demand of you in teaching, life, and conduct of office. A blessed decision! How wonderful!

At the same time you confess to me that you have come to the conviction that the visible Lutheran Church is the church in the proper sense of the word and that the church is to be found nowhere else. In vain I search for a Bible passage in your letter that forces you to this conviction. I simply do not grasp your sudden switch. As resolutely as you want to proceed according to the Word of God, so little can you arrive at that idea. For according to God's Word, the church of Christ is the body of Christ; each member of the church is a member of Christ, of the invisible, spiritual, heavenly Head. The church is subject to Christ, sanctified, cleansed, glorious, without spot, wrinkle, or any such thing, but holy and without blemish (Ephesians 5:23-27). I therefore do not understand how your decision to proceed most scrupulously according to God's Word fits in with your new concept of the church, and how you cannot see that when the Scripture calls visible communities, pure and impure (in doctrine, faith, and life), "churches," it does so according to the familiar synecdoche, according to which often the whole bears the name of the best part and therefore is only improperly named.

Or have you not looked at the Scriptures and have *presumed* that the Symbols are in conformity with the Scripture? In that case I fathom you even less. Just as in the seventh, so in the eighth article of the Augsburg Confession, the church is called an assembly of all believers and saints, that is, indeed if one wants to speak of it, "properly," as Article VIII says. But have you ever seen an assembly of saints? I strongly doubt it; if you did, you must have received a special revelation from God, which, I might add, I do not believe. You see the mass of those about whom you believe that a part of the congregation of believers is among them, coming to the conclusion from their outward characteristics. But you cannot pick out the believers themselves.

Consider first the Apology of Articles VII and VIII of the Augsburg Confession; then that doubt about what the church is according to Lutheran doctrine must disappear, and I think it is proper for us Lutheran preachers, when we are seeking the correct sense of the Augsburg Confession, to seek it in the authentic explanation of the Apology itself. Oh, just read the Apology on this, and if you read it (without preconceived notions), you will be cured quickly of your papistic conceptions of the church. Consider the case presented by the Articles VII and VIII of the Augsburg Confession, such passages as in the Apology on the Mass where we read, "Thus God preserved His *church, that is some saints under the papacy,* so that the Christian church did not entirely perish." There you see how the saints who lived scattered here and there in the midst of the papacy, according to our Confessions, were the church; through them the church itself was preserved.

Consider further what the Smalcald Articles, III, 12, and what the Small and Large Catechisms in the Third Article of the Creed say, and finally what the Preface to the Book of Concord says of the *churches "which certainly do not agree* with us up to now," but which, understanding the Reformers in context, are still called churches.

If you want to make the visible, orthodox church the one, holy, Christian church (indeed, the visible Lutheran Church), then from that moment on you are disarmed over against the Romans and must consequently become [Roman] Catholic. For either there was no visible orthodox before Luther, or the church was prevailed against by the gates of hell, which is impossible; or the papistic Roman church was the church. Since you deny the first *two* sentences according to your present principles, you must accept the last, and so you must become a papist. That you do not want to do – well then, become a Lutheran, and accept the true Christian doctrine of the Lutheran Church on the church, which it sets forth, as an article of faith, as the congregation of the saints which is recognized as existing by the characteristic marks of Word and Sacraments, and as pure and orthodox by the *pure* Word and Sacrament.

If you have such a great desire to get acquainted with Lutheran doctrine and to maintain it and to teach it faithfully, oh, then read Luther's writings. There is no other possible way to find the *Lutheran* doctrine in its purest, brightest, most complete, and most original form (after Scripture) than in *Luther*. It is just plain foolishness to pick a fight over Lutheran doctrine and follow one's own supposition but not go into Luther himself. This is in summary my general advice to you in your present critical situation. Buy Luther's collected writings if you do not have them already, and read them day and night; and if you proceed straightforwardly, not as Luther's master but as Luther's student, you will soon obtain God-given certainty and happiness in your faith and in your relationship to yourself and to the church.

You are, as you write, as concerned to teach correctly as you are to live piously and to see the one thing needful; O my dear friend, how then can you not see that the concept of the church as a communion of the regenerate and renewed who are gathered in the Spirit conforms to the essence of living Christianity while the mechanical conception of the church as a community of the orthodox (they may be converted or unconverted) leads necessarily to a dead Christianity, that is, to no Christianity at all, and to carnal boasting: "Here is the Lord's temple. Here is the Lord's temple." This concept makes people into Pharisees and the kind of Jews, as the Scripture describes them. John 8:33; Matthew 3:9; Romans 2:17-25, cf. vv. 28-29.

Even if you do seriously want to inculcate a true seeking for salvation with fear and trembling, and likewise a zeal for purity of doctrine, you must return to the doctrine of the church as one spiritual community; otherwise you are laying the basis for a dead *opus operatum* and are leading the people, instead of to the internals, to the externals, which a person can have without having a true faith, without being reborn and renewed.

You speak of your apprehension that our Synod is involved more in fighting for pure doctrine than in the practice of true piety and the implanting of true concern for the soul's salvation. It may seem that way to you if you see only what we do polemically. But if you should visit in our congregations, you would see not only that we bear the sword through God's grace but also that we carry the trowel with sincere faithfulness; that we endeavor with our whole hearts to live in continual, true repentance; and that we seek to guide those entrusted to us with complete faithfulness and zeal. That there may be among us some who recognize no other principle than fighting for pure doctrine, who have not experienced true repentance, I dare not dispute; God alone knows. But this is the common aim of all our pastors; we want to be saved through genuine repentance and to bring others to salvation. My dear brother, a person must not judge people according to outward appearances. Some men seem in their outward appearance to be stiff while in their own little chambers and generally in their hearts they are in the midst of a continuous, hot battle and a burning life of prayer. They withdraw, as does the church in general, from the carnal eyes of shortsighted men, for the kingdom of God (or the church) comes not with outward signs; it is within us.

22. *Controversies per se ought not to discourage the believer. In the midst of doctrinal controversies he should maintain a spirit of joy, Walther writes.*

Do not be downhearted because of your controversies! If you could establish your doctrine without such controversies, then it would surely not be the pure Word of God; your controversies are the stocks and bonds [*Aktie*] which you hold for the people of the *ecclesia militans*. May they cause us to learn always to sing better: "Though devils all the world should fill . . . they shall not overpower us. . . . One little word can fell him." No matter how much they despise us on the surface, in their conscience they fear your synod and ours as the only legitimate heirs of the Reformer, who alone have the genuine *successio doctrinalis*. Sinners we are, that is true, but we have not sinned against our opponents, and we have nothing to apologize for to them. . . .

Be on your guard against the spirit of grief, for that is not the Holy

One, no matter how holy and pious he pretends to be; but the Holy Spirit is a spirit of joy.

23. Walther's regard for the Lutheran Confessions is put forth in a long letter with quotations from 17th-century theologians. The priority of the Ecumenical Creeds and the Augustana are evident. Because the letter is addressed to a member of the Tennessee Synod, it is of special value.

Now, you ask me also the following questions:

"1. Are all the Symbolical Books the confession of the Evangelical Lutheran Church? Or

"2. is the Unaltered Augsburg Confession *the confession* of our church in the true sense of the word (emphatically, κατ᾽ ἐξοχήν) and the remaining symbols an explanatory defense of the Augsburg Confession?"

To this I venture to give you the following answer.

Of course, all the Symbolical Books *are* and rightfully are *called* the confession of the Evangelical Lutheran Church. For although specifically the Apology, the Smalcald Articles, and the Formula of Concord have the purpose of repeating, explaining, extending, and defending the Augsburg Confession, this particular purpose does not strip them of their character as public church confessions. For a document to explain and defend a Confession and to be a Confession in its own right is not contradictory. Moreover, it is especially important that we have symbols in which our primary confession is *symbolically* explained and explicated. As a case in point, both of Luther's Catechisms are thoroughgoingly independent confessions. A document becomes a church confession either if it was written for this purpose by the church or if the church elevates a formerly private writing to be its own [confession]. Now there is, of course, no question that all the Symbolic Books of our orthodox church are acknowledged as her public confession of faith, although in certain Lutheran particular [territorial] churches for various reasons only the Unaltered Augsburg Confession is specifically named when its teachers make their confessional oath or pledge. No Lutheran will deny that the Book of Concord contains the Symbols of the Lutheran Church; a church symbol and a confession of the church are of course identical.

Nevertheless among the Symbolical Books of our church there are certain distinctions. The order in which they are presented in the Book of Concord represents the esteem in which they are held by our church. Those that are most highly esteemed by our church are simply the Ecumenical Symbols; however, it regards the Augsburg Confession as its fundamental confession or, as the forefathers liked to say, as the apple of her eye; and so on down to the Formula of Concord. Thus, for example, the famous Leipzig theologian, John Benedict Carpzov, writes in his *Isagoge in libros ecclesiarum Luth. symbolicos* in the year 1675: . . .

> Although, when they (the Symbolical Books) are compared with one another, one does have *priority over the other and yet by no means can one be equated with another* as the Neustädt (Calvinists) have charged us in their admonition. The composers of the Book of Concord wished to indicate this very fact by *the sequence* they observed in arranging the Confessions. For although all are in agreement that no one of the Confessions is the principle of faith, but all are normed by the Scripture, nevertheless there are certain merits that one has over another. For the *Ecumenical* Symbols have the preeminence of antiquity and universality over the other Confessions, in view of which they cannot be made equal to these. The *Augsburg Confession* has priority over the Apology because it was presented to the emperor and accepted prior to it [the Apology]. The *Apology* surpasses the Smalcald Articles in age and also in respect. The *Smalcald Articles* have one point of primacy over Luther's Catechism in that they were drawn up under the authorization of the Protestant estates and confirmed by subscription of the theologians. Therefore all these documents, although all are approved and ratified (confirmed and declared valid) by our churches, nevertheless, *when compared with one another,* have their variations, which is indicated by the sequence and order [in the Book of Concord]. The last to be added to these is the *Formula of Concord,* so-called in the narrower sense, which necessity demanded be appended to the former ones as the authors of the Formula of Concord indicate.

. . . .

It is my concluding judgment, therefore, that even in view of the great superiority which the Augsburg Confession might well have over all the other Lutheran Confessions, it would nevertheless not be right to designate it as "the Confession of the Lutheran Church in the true sense of the word" and to call the others only explications or defenses of this Confession, meaning that the latter are excluded from the Confessions of our church. Of course, I willingly grant that a church can be purely Lutheran, even if it does not specifically obligate its preachers to all the Confessions. A genuinely Lutheran church will obviously not contradict any of the Symbols contained in the Book of Concord. Indeed, *the absence of any official use* of the Symbols written after the Augsburg Confession seems to me to be a *deficiency in the constitution* of a church *and its confessional basis,* although I am far from counseling anyone to press tumultuously for the acceptance of all the

Symbols as the constitutionally *legal* doctrinal basis. Such pressuring makes the most innocent matter suspicious.

Here you have my convictions. May my comments be of some usefulness to you.

May God bind us together more and more intimately on the eternal basis of truth and on the whole truth, and may He bless your beloved synod [the Tennessee Synod], which had grace from God to continue steadfastly in the days when everything in America was unstable.

24. *What is true Lutheranism? It is not a seeking after honor among men, but a readiness to submit to God's will. Walther's sentiments are expressed in commenting on an article that polemicized against the Pennsylvania Ministerium.*

True Lutheranism does not come overnight but is born through travail and the waves of difficult anxieties of conscience and difficult struggles. And above all, only he can be a Lutheran in the true sense of the word who no longer seeks honor before men (John 5:44), for whom it is enough to have God's approval, then leaves it up to God whether He [God] wants to push us forward or whether He wants to leave us small, unnoticed, and forgotten. But that, above all, seems to me to be absent from the dear Pennsylvanians. They would at once concur with the other imposing bodies, and it is unbearable to them if their opponents can point to and look disdainfully on them as if [they are] a small light and at their community as a harmless, small group. But it cannot be otherwise. God's matters always begin disdainfully in human eyes, also a self-renewing church.

25. *The importance of the Scriptures and their proper interpretation were of great concern for Walther. Following correct principles of interpretation would help the theologian in a doctrinal controversy. However, the layman should not be worried about translations of the Bible. The testimony of the Spirit and the truthfulness of the pastors should reassure him about translations that are accepted.*

I hope that my few theses will form the basis on which the entire doctrine of *Sola Scriptura* in all its ramifications may easily be built up and improved. The sharper one defines the simplest rules of hermeneutics the easier the most intricate questions may be blown away like thin wisps of fog. I believe that one is invincible over against all sophists by clinging to those fundamental rules. As soon as one is driven to consternation in even one instance, that is, as we Germans say, if one permits himself to be bluffed, that simply is due to the fact that one does not remain fully conscious of the significance of the most important principles of hermeneutics.

As far as the question is concerned whether the Norwegian Lutheran Church might have approved a translation in a general way, if an obvious error concerning a Scriptural dogma had been contained in them, without thereby having become a sect, I must answer: Indeed! For every church states, with Augustine: "I may err, but I will not be a heretic" *(Errare potero, haereticus non ero)*. It would be a different matter if the fundamental error had not only crept in and had been overlooked but had been defended as God's Word, for then the church by this action would have become a sect. I would not dare to deny the possibility of a mistake, even of a grave error in a translation of the Bible a priori, since this would militate against John 14:26; 16:23, since these promises are given not to a particular church but only to the church as a whole. However, no layman need question the correctness of the translation, though he is not familiar with the original languages, as long as he through the translation has received the testimony of the Holy Spirit, and those whom he has proved to be orthodox teachers give him the assurance that there can be no doubt about the correctness of a certain passage. If he does not want to learn Hebrew and Greek, the last refuge for a layman in case of doubt is a testing according to the analogy of faith.

26. *Walther defines "public" as emanating from the authority of an organized group, not as being performed in a public forum. The context of the definition is a discussion of the pastoral office.*

Publicly to administer the Keys does not mean in public places and the like; but rather, by order of an organized group, in the common interest. . . . Therefore Luther says, regarding the office of preacher or pastor: . . . "St. Paul is at that place speaking about the prophets, who are to teach, and not about the mob, which hears him. If a person will read the entire chapter, he will clearly discover that St. Paul is there speaking of prophecy, teaching, and preaching *in* the congregation or church; *and he does not command the congregation to preach,* but deals with the *preachers,* who are preaching in the congregation or gathering"; . . . naturally, I do not cite this because it entered my mind that you did not already know this or denied it. I merely want to say thereby that in itself it is not incorrect to state that the *public* preaching is exclusively a call and right of the preacher. . . . The church clearly has, as you write, "*all* power of the Keys," but the *manner and way* in which this is used in the public ministerial office originates only from the fact that the congregation or church has the command . . . to elect and appoint people for the exercise of that power in its stead, in the common interest, publicly and in relation to itself; not, however, to do this itself, which would again involve a contradiction, since the church cannot exercise the office "in its stead." . . .

The other thing I noticed in your reply against Diedrich is that you do not want to admit that the pure Word is always the voice of the church, wherever it may sound forth. Why do you want to deny this? Is not a missionary's pure preaching among heathen, Jews, and Turks truly the voice of the church? Is an imperial pardon appearing in Germany not a pardon of the emperor, even though he may be staying in America at the time? Diedrich's appeal is not in itself wrong, but it does not disprove anything.

For our doctrine is this, that wherever God's Word is in common use in a community, there the church does exist by virtue of the never-failing promise of Isaiah 55. . . .

Regarding "action of the church," I believe that a careful distinction must be made between "action of the church" as church and insofar as it is still in the flesh; the former takes place when its action is in obedience to God's Word and command, the other, when it is done regarding earthly matters according to reason and experience, provided that even here it safeguard its freedom from human will.

27. One letter on the Predestinarian Controversy is included in this selection not because predestination or election is a burning issue in the church today but because the controversy was of great consequence for Lutheranism in America after 1880. This letter is an excellent summary of Walther's position and a defense of that position. He also states the position of his opponent fairly but attacks it immediately. He still hoped for reconciliation. The letter is addressed to a member of the Norwegian Synod.

You pose the question "Does your sermon in the *Postille* for the 20th Sunday After Trinity give an exact presentation of your doctrine, as far as it goes?" To this I answer gladly: Yes! This sermon, which I preached in 1852 in the first fervor after I by God's grace became clear about the doctrine of election, contains the doctrine that I still today hold as the only one conforming to the Scriptures and the Confessions.

. . . .

After no one took offense at this, it is therefore foolish to want to

43

call me a heretic, when I forsake the τεόπος παιδείας of the 17th century in the doctrine of predestination (not the doctrine itself) and return to the manner of teaching of the Concordia and generally of the Reformation period. With their τεόπος the dogmaticians wish to reject the *universal and absolute predestination.* I also wish to do that with mine, and on the other hand I believe that the dogmaticians do *not* attain our *common* goal with their doctrine of election "in view of faith, from foreseen faith, preceding faith, and consequent election." True, they are safeguarded from synergism, because they reject the "because of faith, the *generating* cause, which God foresaw"; on the contrary they regard faith purely as an evident work and gift of God. However, with their "in view of faith, from foreseen faith, preceding faith, and following election," they give even the Calvinists a weapon to attack them as synergists, although they are not that, but they merely awaken the appearance of synergism by their τεόπος παιδείας.

The doctrine of "absolute" predestination *is not contained* in this, that the Calvinists place election before faith and make this faith an effect of election, *but in this,* that they teach a *predestination to reprobation.* They reject the universality of the love and grace of God, salvation, and effective calling. They do not admit that any faith in the non-elect flows out of the general gracious will [of God] and from the power of [His] earnest call. They permit faith in the elect to be the fruit of an "irresistible grace."

What the Calvinists reject according to this, we believe with Luther, and what they *maintain* we reject with him. This is certain when we say with Chemnitz: "For God's election does not *follow* faith and our justification but precedes it as the efficient cause." On that account we do not believe in an *irresistible* grace by which according to the Calvinists the elect must come to faith. However, we maintain that the elect and the non-elect come to faith in the same way. [We maintain] therefore that just as the gift of faith is the effect of *common* grace for all men, so is the *special* grace of election, and that accordingly in this respect both are alike.

From this you yourself can guess how I must answer your second question: "Whether I have anything dogmatically against Dr. Philippi when he explains the προέγνω in Rom. 8:29 as 'knew beforehand' but adds thereto that God in His foreknowledge of their (the believers') faith regarded it as nothing else than that *they themselves were His own creation in Christ Jesus,* because otherwise the *free* election would be jeopardized?" I answer that *dogmatically* also I know of nothing to counter against it; yes, I must say that Philippi's formulation is more circumspect than that of most dogmaticians. However, as this out-standing man expresses himself about "the second way of teaching," namely in his *Dogmatics,* I cannot say the same. He tries to justify it as a further extension of the first (Reformational and Confessional). And as far as the interpretation of οὓς προέγνω is concerned, I regard this as unfounded, since the Scripture has οὓς and not την πίστην. To give the proof in refutation requires more than is possible in a letter, since here all passages of the New Testament in which the word προγνώσις would have to be compared. In time we will give the Scrip-tural proof in *Lehre und Wehre.*

. . . .

Enclosure:

The manuscript for the *Lutheraner* of the 1st of March has already gone to the press. In it, sentence 9 reads about as follows:

"We believe, teach, and confess: (1) Predestination is not merely God's foreknowledge; (2) Predestination is not the counsel of God per-taining to all men to redeem the world and to save it; (3) Predestination is not the counsel to save the believers so that also the πρόσκαιροι be-come elect; (4) Predestination is not the bare counsel about the salva-tion of those who believe until the end. Therefore we condemn the opposing Rationalism, Socinianism, Huberianism, Arminianism, Synergism." . . .

Just as I was ready to seal my letter at this enclosure, I received a submitted manuscript from Prof. [A. L.] Graebner in Milwaukee for *Lehre und Wehre.* In it he shows that προέγνω is not to be understood as foreknowledge of faith but as election. Dr. [C. P.] Krauth has al-ready written in the *Lutheran and Missionary* that Prof. Schmidt gave himself a difficult task if he wants to prove that we are Crypto-Cal-vinists. Krauth indeed is correct, and S [chmidt] will come to shame if he doesn't pull in his reins soon. I wish everything good. But he acted most shamefully when he labeled us with the name of the vilest heretics that ever lived. It attacked our doctrine as false without first bringing the matter before the Synodical Conference, to which we both belong. But to give us that shameful name at the same time, that beats everything. May God keep him that *he* does not become a heretic, for "pride is the mother of heresy."

C. F. W. W.

45

IV. About the Pastoral Office

Both as a theologian and as a churchman Walther had to deal with questions concerning the pastoral office, among them the question of ordination. He makes a clear case for the distinction between those called to the office of pastor and those who belong to the royal priesthood. In giving counsel to his brothers in the holy ministry regarding accepting or declining calls, he followed some well-defined principles. Faith and love played a prominent role in his considerations. He stressed the Gospel as the operating principle in the church in respect to an ordination oath. The need for reconciliation with one's brothers is one that must be pervasive for a pastor.

28. Walther rejoiced because his son Ferdinand had been ordained and begun his work in Brunswick, Missouri. Perhaps he knew or sensed that Ferdinand would be depressed and, therefore, gave him advice to be confident and of good cheer.

I have lived to see the oft-coveted time when you are in the holy ministry. You are now ordained to the service of Christ in His church by the old apostolic rite of laying on of hands. That means that the demand is made of you as one vowed to the Lord to have no other goal in this world until your death than to lead souls to the Savior (which He has bought so dearly with His blood), on your part to spread truth and holiness on the earth, and to help to edify the kingdom of God or the church. You are already now beginning this duty and are engaged with the congregation assigned to you.

Oh, what a happy man you will be if you now administer your office faithfully! Your work is the most honorable, the holiest, the most blessed, and the happiest that a man can perform. It also has the most glorious reward, for the teachers are to shine as the splendor of heaven and, in leading many to justification, as the stars for ever and ever. (Dan. 12:3)

Now, indeed, you will say, "Yes, if I am faithful, I can take comfort completely in these promises. However, I am afraid because I have an evil, idle flesh and blood. I even fear that I will not be faithful, and therefore I have to consider more the difficult accounting of a servant to God than the promises given to him."

But, my dear son, the less you trust in your corrupted heart, so much the better. Indeed, you cannot be faithful by your own strength. But each morning bend your knees and ask Him to cleanse your heart, to sanctify it, to fill it with His Spirit, and to urge you on; then God will help you also to overcome yourself and to live only for your holy office. [That office] is heartily to love the souls entrusted to you and to be a good steward of God's mysteries, of God's Word and His holy sacraments. "But," you will probably say, "I am not only too unworthy and too corrupt, I am also too unskilled to do what I am required to do." But consider, the apostle Paul himself cried out: "Who is sufficient for this? Not that we are sufficient for ourselves to think anything as of ourselves, but that our sufficiency is of God." 2 Cor. 2:16; 3:5

Even if you are ever so unqualified, be convinced that the dear Lord Himself has called you Himself and say to God daily and confidently: "You have sent me; oh, make me able now. I would readily have stayed away from this difficult office, but You have directed me through my parents from childhood, so that I had to become Your servant. Oh, help me now to carry out everything well!" Then God will not forsake you nor let you get stuck, but will give you the necessary wisdom in all things. Only let God's Word be your counselor and prayer your refuge. Never do anything hastily! First consider everything carefully! Remain humble and modest over against God and men! To the humble God gives grace, and to the sincere He allows success.

You have received, I understand, a congregation that is like a new land. Don't let that be displeasing to you. It will be much better if you can say: "By His grace the Lord has made this field arable, blooming, green, and fruitful through me." Indeed, in new congregations there are many coarse things that are to be rooted out, but it is much more difficult to direct old congregations, in which are found people with varieties of scruples, false saints, and self-important individuals. Only show your people that you love them and would readily serve them; that you prefer neither rich nor poor, neither the friendly nor the recalcitrant. Be friendly with everyone! Show yourself content with everything, even if you must compel and force yourself! In time things will get better. Also, if one at first has it miserable, so much the better when later on things improve.

29. *Walther congratulated his nephew, John Walther, the son of his deceased brother Hermann, on his ordination. This letter points up the high regard Walther had for the Gospel ministry.*

May the Lord Jesus equip you more and more to be a truly loving matchmaker, who tirelessly woos for Him the souls dearly bought by Him! Yes, it is true that sooner than you think you will find many, many unlovely souls. However, only recall that the Lord saw them lying in much greater filth, yes, polluted in their own blood, and yet He had only mercy for them and said, "You shall live." Ezekiel 16:1-6. Yes, He cleansed them "with the washing of water by the Word." [Eph. 5:26] Make the merciful Savior your Master and think less about how you will act according to correct procedure than how you will begin to win, to rescue, to save.

30. *Walther advises an unidentified pastor to accept a call to a congregation in Chicago. In doing so, he defines a "divine call." He warns the called pastor about the changes he will experience in carrying out his duties in Chicago.*

First, what makes you doubtful about the call to Chicago is, as you write, your frailty, which you fear would not permit you to fulfill the obligation of the many sermons and talks that would be required in Chicago. Also you think that the fund of your professional experience would be insufficient for the cases that occur in such a large congregation.

Here I must call to your attention that your call has all the characteristics of a divine call. You have in no wise sought it. Others, who after all also have good judgment and fear God, have proposed you. The congregation, which knows little or nothing about you, has in a wonderful manner given you its confidence. All this and more, which I will not mention for the sake of brevity, puts it beyond doubt that the Lord is calling you, *and you must simply hold to this in childlike faith!* He will be mighty in your weakness.

You must also consider that up to now you were burdened with a school, and naturally preaching could not be easy for you. But since you will not have to teach school in Chicago, you will soon notice how advantageous that is for preaching. You can apply all your energy to sermon making, and you will not have to get at it after you have labored in the school until you are tired and worn out and have almost consumed your spiritual and physical powers.

31. The particular situation in Buffalo, New York, early in 1867 prompted Walther to urge Ruhland to stay there. The colloquy between the Missouri and Buffalo synods had been held late in November and early December in 1866. Only reasons of health would be compelling enough for Ruhland to accept a call away from Buffalo at this time.

Without a doubt your present position is a great deal more important than that to which you are being called. Hardly a post may be found in our Synod that makes greater demands than your present one for clear understanding, common sense, psychological insight, a knowledge of human nature, energy, flexibility, patience, love, perseverance, etc., etc. Consequently you could leave with a clear conscience only if you must say that you were given by God less of all these qualities than all those [qualities] your eventual successor must have. But that I must most certainly deny. If you go, I know of nobody to propose in your stead. And not only that I know of no suitable man but I also know of no one who could replace you; not to mention the great gain that you have gathered through your many years of activity in Buffalo in the knowledge of the people themselves, of their attitudes, of their peculiarities, of their good and bad sides, and of all the relationships there; and not to mention the experience you have acquired in dealing with the people there. All of that a newly called pastor lacks, and he must gain that just as you had to, through many bitter experiences.
. . . .

In summary: I vote for your staying. If I were to participate, only *one* argument would silence me, that your health did not permit you to administer so large a congregation. However, I fear that you may worry a little more about the minute circumstances with their annoying trivia than the large obstacles which you have overcome in Buffalo. You write freely of the "disgust" at the conduct there, but look for that confidently in your flesh and not in your spirit. God would have had many more reasons to be disgusted at the whole of mankind, yet He descended and put up with the horrible parish of Judea with its affiliates in Samaria and Galilee to death, even the death on the cross. If all this does not convince you, then consider it as not written, and throw this page into the fire. But I still deal honestly with you, right?

32. This letter in which Walther advises a pastor in the matter of accepting or declining a call shows his keen analytical sense and his devotion to the welfare of the church.

Frequent leaving of congregations and acceptance of others is a great hindrance to establishing congregations in a Christian ethos. It is indeed certain that God not only places but also displaces His servants. Nevertheless, the concomitant question remains whether a pastor should regard another call as divine and to be accepted. He must proceed by weighing all the circumstances with great earnestness, and he must decide in such a manner that he does not succumb to a temptation accoutred in a call.

Since all gifts are given for the common good, he will consider above everything else, therefore, if essentially he can use his gifts, according to all human calculations, more profitably for Christ's kingdom in the congregation that is calling away than in the congregation where he is. Furthermore, since every congregation is a member of a larger body, he should give consideration not only for this member but at the same time for the entire body to which it in a lesser or greater degree belongs.

Now if I apply this principle, which is without doubt Biblical, to your case, I see, first, that your congregation in Lyons has 25 voting and 10 contributing members. In 1875 the congregation in Baden had 21, in 1876 it had 19 voting members. I do not know how many now, but to judge from the past the membership in the congregation at Baden would scarcely equal the members at Lyons. Baden, therefore, decidedly is not a place whose call is more urgent than the call in which you now function. I would be genuinely happy, it is true, if God would so direct things that you would be closer to us. I also regard it as entirely natural that you long to leave your isolated theological situation. Only, that cannot be decisive; for I cannot, other things being equal, shake off something unpleasant, which another must then assume.

Finally, you must also take into consideration the welfare of the body to which Lyons belongs as a more intimate member, the new Iowa District to be organized. We dare not weaken (allow me to say this) this weak District instead of strengthening it in every way. Whoever in this District is more able than others to put his shoulder to the wheel for the general upbuilding ought then to be called away or go away only because of an evidently divine indication. I would gladly have nominated you quite often, but I could not reconcile my conscience to depriving Iowa of you, where, for one thing, God has now placed you. My firm conviction, therefore, is that you should not go to Baden.

As far as Dubuque is concerned, it consists of 27 voting members, Lyons of 25, excluding 10 contributing. In Dubuque 4 were buried

50

in one year; in Lyons, 12. In Dubuque there were 3 marriages; in Lyons, 9. In Dubuque there are 30 pupils in [the parish] school; 35 in Lyons. For one thing, there can be no talk according to these statistics of a place requiring greater gifts for the [pastoral] office, which Dubuque supposedly is. That the Iowans have an opposition [congregation] in Dubuque does not seem to me, in weighing the mutual demands of the two places, as sufficient [reason] for regarding it as God's will that you should sever the bond that binds you to Lyons. It will not be more difficult to obtain a pastor for Dubuque than for Lyons, if you should leave there. Briefly, the call to Dubuque is not essentially stronger than the call you already have; in such a case, it seems to me, staying is always the most certain.

To all this, however, must be added yet that you will still be loaded down with teaching school, whether you go to Baden or Dubuque; this virtually deprives you of the opportunity for further theological studies. I think, therefore, that only then the time will have come for you to take up your staff when you have received a call to a larger congregation in which the school is separate from the pastoral office; and even in that case you will still have to take into consideration whether you should remain to assist Iowa or not. —

Content yourself with this little bit. May God enlighten and govern you to recognize His will and to act for your own welfare and for the furtherance of the work of God in the redeemed world.

33. Walther advises a pastor to accept a call to Houston, assuring him that his gifts are needed there. Misgivings that he might have about himself or what enemies in Houston might say should not deter him.

Based on detailed reports about conditions in Houston, which I have received from various quarters, it is my firm opinion that the call extended to you is a call from God. With the situation in Houston as it is, there is definitely no need for a man who has a special talent to attract the masses by his fiery eloquence. Those who called you are in need of clear and thorough teaching, evangelical treatment, faithfulness in pastoral care, calm, considerate, careful behavior and conduct, publicly and privately. By the grace of God you are better able to offer them this than others are. . . .

Because you too greatly underestimate the gifts God has given you, you have now hesitated long enough to heed the Lord's call. I therefore venture to beg you very earnestly to leave without delay to pitch your tent in the oft-mentioned city.

The Lord be with you! Not only the prayers of your new congregation sustain you but also those of all your co-workers who longingly look for the moment when you will lift your voice in Houston among a diseased fold of famished and abandoned sheep of Christ.

34. A short paragraph in a letter to an unidentified pastor, in which Walther dealt with other practical questions, encourages seeking advice but making one's own decision.

Concerning being called away, you should not let your decision depend entirely on the judgment of others, otherwise you might fall into difficulties of conscience. Those are two different things, to act independently as a know-it-all in such matters, and to get advice from others and in the final analysis to make one's own decision. The latter is the right [thing]. But, to be sure, you do not seem to be helped if indeed you receive another ministerial office but still have to continue teaching [school].

35. Walther's advice to the students of the Norwegian Synod at Concordia Seminary about swearing to the ordination oath, imposed on all who were ordained in Norway and used within the Norwegian Synod, had to be explained. Basically Walther's objections came from a fear of giving church officials too much power. The president of a church body, he says, is only the first among equals.

Now as for the oath!
My opinion is indeed this, that a promise in the form of an oath is more a matter for the state than for the church; since the rule in the church is not done through the Law as letter, but through the Gospel and by love; therefore, the church must be satisfied with the mere promise. It is only in the state that the oath brings about an end of all strife, as a species of torture which certainly is to the advantage of the state, Heb. 6:16, since the state has in mind not so much conscience as quiet and peace, and renders judgment not so much according to love as according to the law as letter. It is for this reason that Luther writes: "The word *perjured* belongs only to worldly things (where oaths are sworn and demanded), not to spiritual or divine things." But although this is my conviction and I therefore believe that your oath has its basis in the fact that the Norwegian Church was state church, I still would not, *caeteris paribus,* consider it wrong to swear an oath also in this matter, if I were a Norwegian, for I do not consider it a sin, inasmuch as the oath is a *res media.*
As far as the wording of the oath is concerned, I, in the first place,

object to the words: *"Ceremoniae in ecclesia receptae observentur, nec quidquam contra constitutiones ecclesiasticas admittatur."* If this were an oath taken in the state church, a conscience might be able to bear it, since the oath is demanded by the secular government; one indeed had to take it in order to agree with the command of God to be subject to the government that has power over us in all things, sinful matters alone excepted. It is another matter with regard to an autonomous church; since such a one does not have the power to make laws that bind consciences, she also has not power to demand an oath in matters indifferent, namely, beyond what love may demand. To this must be added that I do not see how this part of the oath could be kept here in America. In place of the sentence given above I take the liberty, without any specific authority, to suggest the following substitute taken from the Formula of Concord: *"Omnia decenter et bono ordine fiant nect quidquam cum levitate et scandalo contra constitutiones ecclesiasticas admittatur."*

Furthermore I object to the words: *"Non passurum ullum affluere . . . liceat."* Since the vow has the force of an oath, I should judge that a conscientious person could thereby come into terrible scruples of conscience. The passage seems to me to be a snare for consciences. Yet as strongly as I would vote in favor of its being stricken, this would still not be a *conditio sine qua non* of taking the oath.

Finally, I object to the words: *"Velim meo episcopo, ut et praeposito, omne licitum obsequium praestare, imperata paratissimo animo facere."* Why? does not require any exposition. The *"licitum"* is indeed a restriction of the obedience, but one which is to be made also relative to the secular government. According to this provision the bishop or provost or president would clearly have governmental authority in ecclesiastical matters, a condition that does not hold true in an autonomous church, in which he is not incidentally the government but a *primus inter pares*. This is true also of the word *"imperata."* Things of this kind simply do not exist in the church as such, outside of God's commands. Matt. 23:8-11; 20:25-28; 2 Cor. 8:8; 1 Peter 5:3. Hence my suggestion would be that the sentence should be changed in some manner, as follows: *"Velim meis praepositis evangelicum obsequium praestare."*

36. In his capacity as president of the Missouri Synod Walther complied with a request from an unknown pastor for a certificate of ordination. He had left the fellowship of the Synod, and Walther directs some harsh words to him, yet showing a deep concern for his spiritual welfare. The anonymity of the person addressed focuses the attention more sharply on Walther's concern.

At your request I asked Dr. S. to draw up an ordination certificate for you. I have now received it and herewith transmit it to you.

You complain about the hardness and lovelessness which you supposedly experienced from us. I am sorry to see from this that you are still captured by the self-deception that did not allow you to see the matter in its right light already in _____. I can assure you that in the entire process against you so far as I am concerned, both in the latest dealings and in the written report about you, nothing motivated me but love to your immortal soul and the dearly bought souls that were entrusted or might possibly be entrusted to you.

I must therefore testify to you again that your whole attitude has convinced me that now you no *longer* belong to those who have surrendered their souls for the name of our Lord Jesus Christ, that you rather bear a relation to those in Phil. 2:20-21. Hence I cannot tell you how much it hurts me that I cannot be one in the fellowship of love with a person like you with whom I once knew myself at one in doctrine.

37. Pastors should remain true to the Confessions of the Lutheran Church, Walther writes. He is willing, as president of Concordia Seminary, to supply a promising area with a candidate, but he outlines carefully what the relations of a congregation to its pastor should be. He adds an encouragement to continue faithfulness to the church.

I rejoiced with all my heart to learn from it that also in your remote North the Lord is beginning to stir up souls, so that a place might be prepared there for the pure Gospel as God once caused it to be preached again by His faithful servant Luther. God bless and prosper this godly project! It is certain that one whose only concern is to have a church without asking whether the old, unadulterated Gospel is being preached there is helping the erection of the tower of Babel which is being built so zealously here in America by a hundred sects.

All sects rise and fall like comets, but only the star of our dear orthodox church of the Unaltered Augsburg Confession will continue to shine, even though a cloud now and then hides it from view. For: "God's Word and Luther's doctrine pure shall to eternity endure"; "The Word they still shall let remain, nor any thanks have for it. He's by our side upon the plain with His good gifts and Spirit." No matter how much our Lutheran Catechism is despised, it nevertheless is and remains a fortress which can be captured as little as the world can storm the fortress of the Bible. For while in other catechisms of the sects there are various rationalistic additions, the mine shaft of our precious Catechism contains nothing but the pure gold and the sterling, seven times purified and tested, precious ore of divine truth.

God give you strength to hold high this flag of our church in your area, so that all the straying children of our church may there reassemble under her banner, and many others may come and join us in confessing the one faith in one love and hope. . . .

Since I now see clearly how important the Rock Island-Davenport area is, I will gladly do my part so that you will get a man who is not after the wool but after the sheep and who is capable of establishing something solid. But, alas, I can hardly furnish you such a man before the beginning of May. In April five students will have completed their theological studies here, and they then should enter into the Lord's vineyard. You could extend a call to one of these. I am convinced that you would then be well supplied. . . . Only I must tell you in advance that you can receive such a candidate only if you would call him on the basis of God's Word and the confessional writings of our church. We will not permit our preachers to be turned into servants of men. For that reason we will not allow them to be hired for a year or for several years, but with unspecified tenure, as long as the Lord wills, that is, as long as the preacher faithfully discharges his office or until he is called away or until God summons him through death. This is not to say that a congregation could not get rid of our preachers under any circumstances. If a preacher becomes a false teacher, that is, if he departs from the pure Gospel or if he is not faithful in his office or if he leads a scandalous or even offensive life, the congregation can depose him from his office. A further condition: Our preachers will receive into the congregation and admit to Holy Communion only those who believe in the Word of God and desire to be Lutherans and lead a Christian life. We want nothing to do with syncretism and a false union of churches. Furthermore, our preachers will admit no one to Holy Communion except those who have announced their intention beforehand, for we do not want to give what is holy to dogs nor throw pearls before swine, something that the Lord has so earnestly forbidden. The people must not think that we want to lord it over them in this way, for we heartily detest all priestly domination and all clerical dictatorship; we have already been compelled to fight against that a great deal and to suffer much because of it. But we do aim also at gathering regular Lutheran congregations that rest on a firm foundation, not a vagabond rabble that holds together today and scatters tomorrow. According to the constitution of our Synod a preacher may not give orders to a congregation; he is simply to preach God's Word and demand obedience to it. In other matters, such as church orders and the like, the congregation has freedom. Here the preacher can only offer his good advice, and the majority of the voting members (that is, those who are on the membership roster and have reached the age of 21) adopts valid resolutions.

38. *Two extant letters by Walther to J. C. W. Lindemann reveal that Lindemann did not agree with Walther's position that teachers in a parish school held an office that was derived from the pastoral office. He points to his own writings in an attempt to dissuade Lindemann.*

Your letters please me extremely well, and I consider them to be excellently suited for publication in the *Lutheraner*. However, I cannot convince myself that the teachers who teach God's Word in their schools do not have a churchly office and are not the helpers of the pastor, but rather as private persons should merely assist in the office of the father of a family. At least I find in our old [writers] the opposite, although naturally the school office, just like the preaching and magisterial office, flows out of the patriarchal office, if we go back to the first source of all estates.

My plea to you is, therefore, that you reconsider the matter once again, and if you can convince yourself that I am right, then revise the paragraph in which you polemicize against the teacher's office as a branch office of the pastorate. It does not seem to me that, in doing this, your admonitions and warnings are weakened in any way, nor do they lose their good foundation. Compare thesis VIII of the second part of the book *Church and Ministry* as well as *The Right Form*, pp. 99 – 101. Also see what Luther writes about "the three holy orders and estates" in the beginning of his "Great Confession Concerning Christ's Supper."

39. *After Lindemann became director of the Teachers Seminary in Addison, he still maintained his earlier view. The matter was of considerable importance to Walther. Nevertheless, he permitted Lindemann to hold his view, but he warns him not to cause a disturbance in the church on this point. Peace within the church was of greater importance than conformity in this doctrine.*

What's gotten into you? You yourself demand that I suspend you from office because you cannot perceive what status should be given to a Christian teacher in the church! or rather, because you probably differ with the great majority of the members of our Synod in this connection. This is not a point that would justify such steps; provided, naturally, that for this reason you yourself do not try to cause division and agitation in the church. The only thing that strikes me is that you yourself lay so much weight on this point. Besides that, I am convinced that an oral discussion would soon cause you to agree with us. Only do everything you can to be sure that a fire will not grow out of a little spark. For Satan has at times begun with less significant matters when he wanted to plunge the church into unnecessary struggle.

40. *Leaning heavily on Luther, Walther instructed Pastor Ottesen of the Norwegian Synod about the difference between the pastoral office and the laity. Walther sees himself stressing the rights of the laity in the situation in which he found himself, while Ottesen had to uphold the pastoral office in his situation.*

What Luther wishes to prove with 1 Cor. 14 in the essay of 1523 remains true after as well as before. Luther teaches: The Keys or the office belong originally and immediately [*unmittelbar*] to the whole church, that is, to all believers. But God has established the ordinance in the church that this office is to be administered publicly only by those especially called to it, who are competent to teach, and who now in a special sense by virtue of their office can in the name and command or in the stead of Christ function publicly.

However, because the church originally has the office, every Christian can and should make use of this privilege, where His [God's] ordinance is not disrupted thereby, for example, among the heathen, or where necessity cancels the ordinance, e. g., when no pastor is available to baptize a dying child, or when a wolf opens his mouth in the church, every Christian then has the power, yes, the duty and the obligation to oppose him. This doctrine, which Rasmussen's practice condemns, pervades the entire Luther, and there is no statement of Luther's, either in his earlier or his later years, which would contradict it. Whether Luther based this doctrine at different times in various ways doesn't make any difference as far as the question is concerned. Granted that Luther's earlier explanation of 1 Cor. 14 is to be preferred to his later one, this would not alter the matter in the least; for in that writing he proves only that the office is no such monopoly for the tonsured [*Beschorenen*], that it could not be administered either among unbaptized heathen or in case of necessity also by a layman. But who denies this? This is applicable then to Apollos, in whose case there is also this circumstance, that he clearly possessed an immediate enlightenment or, for all that, that he was furnished with extraordinary gifts, which were peculiar only to the apostolic era. Only stupidity and maliciousness can maintain that Spener had a different doctrine and developed it in his tract on the spiritual priesthood.

Concerning students and candidates who also preach occasionally, this example is a bad resource. For they preach for the very purpose that the ordinance of the ministerial office be retained, not that it be upset; their sermons are exercises, preparations, and examinations for the purpose of future appointment and induction into the ministerial office. They do this therefore not as laymen. . . . Besides that, their sermons are first scrutinized and examined. They therewith cite [*sistiren*] themselves, so to speak, for election by the church.

When the essay *Kirche und Amt,* page 24, says: "A layman shall not presume to teach in the presence of bishops, except when they themselves request it of him," this does not say that there could not be cases in which such a demand is justified. Who will deny that there could be such cases! The question is whether such an arrangement might be made according to which the pastor would grant the layman as a right occasionally to teach the people publicly in his stead and to lead them publicly in prayer, and when this is done customarily. Such action is so absolutely diametrically opposed to the Scriptural doctrine of the office (1 Cor. 12:29; Acts 6:4; Titus 1:5) and to Article XIV of the Augsburg Confession, to all testimonies of pure teachers and against the constant practice of our church, that we cannot comprehend how a person who is otherwise grounded in God's Word and fairly well at home in the orthodox church can for one moment be in confusion. To base such a matter on the spiritual *priesthood* of Christians is nonsense, for if that procedure were followed, nobody would have any reason to pay any attention to the calling of the pastor [*Herr Pfarrer*]. Much less can such a procedure be based on a special *call,* for the church cannot create a call according to its own discretion but can issue only that call which God has instituted and which He alone recognizes (through which alone a servant of God comes into existence, not, however, through a human contract for a few hours and days). Moreover, the matter cannot be founded, as is clear, on a case of *necessity.*

May God give you good courage in your destined struggle! While *we* must defend the rights of Christians principally against hierarchy and priestly domination, to you it is perhaps ordained to guard God's ordinance against Enthusiasm. Well, then, therefore in God's name go at it with a will! Your foe is the devil, who often surrounds himself with a halo. Therefore be confident and courageous! It is, of course, a great honor to contend for the truth and to be allowed to suffer disgrace. By all means, do not let yourself be beguiled by Satan to infringe on the rights of Christians for the sake of the Enthusiasts. Keep in mind, the way of true doctrine is narrow. God be eternally thanked that we have behind us a whole cloud of witnesses! We want to join their train. Shall we be victorious? Yea, as truly as the Lord liveth! The gates of hell shall not overpower His church.

God have mercy on poor Rasmussen! It will be easy to dispose of the miserable General Synod people and their stupid impertinence. Naturally, it will cost blood. But as Luther writes about the spirit of the Anabaptists: "Let them preach boldly and briskly whatever they can and against whom they will; for, as I have said, there *have* to be sects, 1 Cor. 11:19, and the Word of God must take to the battlefield and fight. Because of that the evangelicals are called hosts, Ps. 68:11; and Christ, the Lord of hosts, in the prophets. If *their* spirit is right, he will not be afraid of us nor of anybody. Let the spirits clash against one another and strike. *If meanwhile some will be deceived, well, then, that's the way it goes in warfare: where there is strife and fighting, there some must fall and be wounded.* But whoever fights honorably will be crowned."

V. About Congregational Problems

Walther's letters are filled with pastoral counsel to pastors about problems within their congregations. Excommunication was a matter that immigrants from a country dominated by a state church had difficulty comprehending. Walther's advice cautioned pastors against legalistic measures.

There were other questions, e. g., regarding Baptism, confirmation, confession, the necessity of a constitution for a congregation, how Communion is to be administered, fairs, saloons, lotteries and raffles, admitting a layman to the congregation who believed in chiliasm, liturgical innovations, ceremonies, and the like.

Walther's common sense, his readiness to account for weaknesses, patience, and Gospel kindness are evident in these letters.

41. Who must be excommunicated? Only the manifest sinner, answers Walther. A hypocrite must be dealt with as Christ dealt with Judas.

It is scarcely possible for me to take up the details, which you shared with me, since I would have to inquire about much before I could give a sure verdict. Therefore, I can give you advice only in a summarized fashion.

Only very manifest sins can be objects of church discipline, those that must eventually lead to suspension and excommunication. We may be morally persuaded that someone is a Judas without being able to initiate church discipline, so long as this Judas is not so manifest that we must unmask him before all his codisciples. If a person extricates himself by lies and hypocrisy so that we cannot prove it to him before everyone, while the spiritual judgment we have nevertheless tells us that [he is a Judas], then we can do nothing but to tell the liar and hypocrite that we fear that he is not acting with integrity and that we are sharpening his conscience concerning this. However, then we must give such persons over to God's judgment, while naturally we intercede for them for mercy and deliverance. Judas is an important example for the care of souls and church discipline. For Christ, although He was omniscient, dealt with him [Judas] as if He [Christ] were only a man, in order to be an example for us.

42. *Do not be in a hurry to carry out an excommunication, says Walther, if it will disturb the peace of the congregation. The weakness of the people must be taken into consideration. "Formal excommunication belongs not to the essence but to the well-being of the church," he writes.*

I can hardly contain my anger when I hear what congregations in their lack of understanding often demand of a young pastor. God grant that you may not succumb and wear yourself out before your time.

Concerning the matter of excommunication, it is my opinion that you should not push it to extremes. If there would be danger that the congregation would be violently disturbed by carrying out the excommunication as it should be carried out, then refrain from carrying it out, if you will not be forced to give the Sacrament to those who obviously deserve to be excommunicated. A person must, according to the judgment of our fathers, rather let a guilty man pass unnoticed than risk a number of innocent men through the carrying out of thorough church discipline. Formal excommunication belongs not to the essence but to the τò εὖ εἶναι, i. e., to the good arrangement of the church. In the Formula of Concord it is even regarded as an error of the Schwenkfelders if a man teaches "that a congregation in which public expulsion or orderly process of excommunication does not take place is not a true Christian congregation" (Solid Declaration XII). Certainly you do not dare permit the doctrine of excommunication to be taken away from you or even to let yourself be silenced.

But you must explain to the people that you will give way to them because of their weakness until they arrive at a better understanding. Until then the public proclamation in the church, along with the exclusion of the guilty, should be put off. Here again you have an example of how necessary it is to preach diligently about the decay which has taken place in ecclesiastical affairs in Germany, so that the people stop appealing to Germany in their perversity.

43. *Walther commends a pastor for the way in which he handled a question in conjunction with the board of elders and the congregation. An evil misdeed is committed against the pastor, the congregation, against a family, and against the Gospel. The latter is of greatest consequence.*

I am perfectly convinced by your explanation that in every respect you handled the matter correctly, conscientiously, and with the necessary circumspection. You spared me a motivation for agreeing in my judgment with you by your extensive explanation. [It is] for me anything but disagreeable, rather it is very valuable, interesting, and enriching for my own experience.

I would be genuinely sorry if you were to entertain the least suspicion against dear brother M., as if he had somehow made you suspect in his letter to me. That is not the case. M's letter was rather an expression of brotherly and collegial love for you and arose only from tenderness of conscience in a matter in which he would just as soon deal with you in complete harmony.

Without my reminder you will surely do everything to win back R. and will try to soften as much as possible the repentance of the poor slave of his wife, since, as you say, with him alone there might be something to take up. If he wishes to maintain adamantly that he is right and will not answer for his evil misdeed that he committed against you, the congregation, his family, and above all against the Gospel, then nothing else can result under the circumstances than excommunication or an announcement that he has excommunicated himself. I am heartily pleased to see that you have handled this affair in full agreement and in cooperation with your congregation, in particular, the board of elders. They will finish it without a doubt in that way if it has not been done already.

44. *Walther seems to come close to Donatism in the following excerpt about rebaptizing a child, making the rebaptism dependent on the character of the congregation. Since none of the circumstances are known, one must rely on Walther's general principle that the clear nonchurch character of a pastor's congregation casts doubt on the validity of a baptism.*

The preacher in the pulpit is the voice of the congregation that he serves. If the former pastor was a believer and professed the faith, then the congregation at the time was truly one in which baptism had validity, not a nonchurch. First when the believing pastor was driven out by a rabble faction in the congregation and through the dominance this faction finally managed to acquire in the congregation, the congregation has *become* a school of Satan. You ought not to rebaptize the particular child that was baptized by him, whether publicly or privately, for its baptism was valid.

45. *A pastor who wanted some adults to be confirmed publicly ran into resistance and turned to Walther for advice. Walther told him that confirmation was not essential; instruction in the Word was. At the same time he advises him about allowing as sponsors those who were notoriously non-Christians. Such lukewarmness was of no service to the church. Weak Christians can be admitted as sponsors. Walther adds a word of encouragement to his letter.*

To your questions the following may briefly serve as answer. One must not insist in all instances on a formal confirmation of older, already married persons, since confirmation is not by divine law, but a wholesome ecclesiastical ordinance, therefore an adiaphoron or a thing indifferent. Only that which confirmation accomplishes — namely, such a level of wholesome knowledge as is necessary for a worthy and blessed use of the Lord's Supper — only that is by divine law, and no one can or should be dispensed from it. That those who are not confirmed were "confirmed by God" by being permitted to go to the Holy Supper, and therefore are to be dispensed from confirmation, sounds odd. . . .

If I were in your position, I would therefore insist that the persons who have not been confirmed at the very least memorize the text of the Catechism and receive instructions so that they are able to give an account and answers about the chief parts and that they can demonstrate that they have comprehended the doctrine of salvation in its most essential particulars. If they do not want to agree to this minimum in spite of every friendly remonstrance, then you must let them go as people who do not regard themselves as worthy of eternal life. People who so little desire to be furthered in the right knowledge would also hardly receive the Holy Supper other than unworthily and to their damnation. You also remark correctly that here others should also be taken into consideration. If one would give in to such stubborn people, then all Christian discipline and order and the God-pleasing use of the holy sacraments would soon disappear, and also the better minded would easily be harmed severely.

There is no doubt that you cannot allow as sponsors such Free Masons, as you describe them, or other notorious unbelievers, drunkards, whoremongers, and the like. This would mean to be a partaker of the sins of others, and that of a very horrible sin, the desecration of the sacrament. In such a case you must necessarily commit the consequences to God. Even if members of the family who now belong to the congregation would then turn their backs to it, you must comfort yourself with this, that not you, but obedience to God's Word, drove them out of the church.

Lukewarmness often seems initially to serve for a greater furtherance of the church. However, afterwards, it manifests itself as a force that destroys or kills a congregation. In the same way a straight course, where God's Word and honor require it, often seems initially to bring sure ruin to the church. Afterwards it is evident that the storm indeed bent the tree but did not break it; instead it drove its roots deeper into the earth and thus made it a more fruitful tree.

In regard to those who, as far as men can see, left the church under your predecessors because of a lack of knowledge and with an erring conscience and yet withal have the earmarks of upright Christians, I would say that such should not absolutely be denied the right to be sponsors. If this were done, they would be totally estranged from the Lutheran Church. However, if they are accepted as sponsors and are anxious to be [sponsors], then we can hope the sooner to win them.

Yet, it is something entirely different if people leave the congregation because they do not repent of manifest sins; and because they do that, that then those who are confused by wrong doctrine leave the congregation. *Duo cum faciunt idem, non est idem,* that is, "When two do the same thing, it is nevertheless not the same thing."

46. *The following letter dates from 1847. It shows the resistance among lay people of Perry County, Missouri, to bind themselves by the adoption of a constitution. Walther's advice to Pastor Schieferdecker allows the congregation to function without a formal constitution.*

My innermost conviction is that because of God's will you must not jeopardize the continuation or even the expansion of your congregation and your circle of activity by insisting on a *form* of order. If God has opened you a door by the voluntary departure of a false teacher, you can be certain that the devil will plot intrigues to lock this door for you. He does this evidently by making the people anxious because of the subscription they are supposed to make for the proposed constitution. A constitution that would cause disorder and disruption is no longer an order but a disorder. Throw it into the fire! Don't require anything more than a confession to the doctrine and the promise to conduct one's self according to God's Word and to be judged according to it. Those well-intentioned people, who would gladly help but do not want to raise a finger unless a constitution is there, are to be instructed, warned, requested, and begged to give in. The objective is noble, but the matter is after all only human. God holds the hearts in His hand. If God does not help, the constitution can even be without any benefit, but the Word cannot and therefore will not return void.

But don't be churlish against the people, so that they perceive that nothing is under consideration except that the light is in its place and that all permit themselves to be enlightened. Between us, I would rather let those who insist on a human order, than those who do not want to permit a form to be imposed on them, even if from an incorrect understanding; for "to whom much is given, etc." The greater insight of the former, the more ought they be resigned when it comes to advice based on human wisdom.

47. Walther's letter about the giving of the consecrated elements into the hand or the mouth treats the broader aspects of "things indifferent." His quaint exegesis of John 19:28-30 is offset by his use of Galatians 2 to uphold Christian liberty. His readiness to go to the Confessions and to the Lutheran dogmaticians is evident in the letter.

Whether the communicants are given the consecrated elements in the mouth or in the hand is clearly an adiaphoron, a thing indifferent, since Christ neither commanded nor forbade anything about this. To be sure, it is customary in the Lutheran Church to give the elements into the mouth. It has every right to do so, since it is also said of Christ that He "received" the vinegar, although it was held right at His mouth and He could not take the sponge filled with vinegar into His hands while nailed to the cross, without performing a miracle. See John 19:28-30.

In any case it would be well that no congregation that wants to be Lutheran abandon this custom but that all be in conformity. However, since this matter is a thing indifferent, it is in itself not necessary.

There are indeed cases also in things indifferent in which one dare not give way, namely when the things indifferent are forced on one or abolished for the endorsement of error, as discussed in Article X of the Formula of Concord. Therefore when Paul saw that the Jews, beset with their prejudices, would not listen to him if he came with an uncircumcised companion, he had Timothy circumcised because of their weakness, since at that time circumcision was still a thing indifferent. Compare Acts 16:1-3. However, where the false teachers wanted to insist that Titus be circumcised in order to substantiate their false doctrine that also Christians are bound to keep Mosaic law, then he [Paul] did not yield in this adiaphoron "by subjection, no, not for an hour, that the truth of the Gospel might continue with you." Gal. 2:1-5.

Therefore we Lutherans do not give place to the Reformed when they demand that we break the bread in the Holy Supper. They demand this of us as necessary because they want to substantiate their teaching that the Lord's Supper is only a meaningful, symbolical representation of Christ's suffering and death.

Likewise we do not yield to the Rationalists, as also it happened in Hanover, when they demanded the omission of the Apostles' Creed and the renunciation of the devil in Baptism. Here the adiaphoron is connected also with witnessing to pure doctrine.

Therefore, you can see that you should not give up your congregation but yield to it concerning the manner of distributing the consecrated elements. The people are insisting on it because of habit, weakness, and ignorance. One should therefore give in to them, until they come to a clearer understanding.

48. *Walther's letter about fairs with their lotteries, auctions, donations of goods and services, and raffling is broadly tolerant. "Love must not be violated" is his guiding principle.*

Regarding the Fair affair, you certainly did right in protesting against it in the form it existed in Boston. Above all, let me remind you that in your activity against this American custom, you must carefully distinguish the sinful from that which is not in good taste or completely indifferent. The lottery is certainly sinful; the auction is in bad taste. Everything else is indifferent.

I would plead and request that the lottery be dropped, and if it continues, I would withdraw myself completely from the whole affair.

I would counsel against the auction only because it is in bad taste. It is not good when one forces another to bid higher by bidding against one another or when, due to no bidding, a person receives an item below its value. But I would not withdraw because the auction is continued, since it is not wrong in principle. It all depends on how it is used.

Concerning the rest of the things that take place at the Fair Institute, I would not say a word. It certainly is not wrong if someone wants to make a contribution to the church and therefore makes something and, in a manner previously arranged, changes it into money. Some individuals can do this more easily than to give a cash contribution. Only we must see to it that no one has scruples of conscience about it and that no one is forced to buy something he does not want.

I would not use the argument that no command or example of fairs can be found in Scripture. As long as love is not violated by the things connected with it but rather regulated according to love, there is no need of a specific example or command. In general, I would not treat this matter too seriously. Even about the raffling, an individual may not experience its sinfulness, because he participates more for fun than for profit and is therefore as satisfied to lose as to win. Of course, such an individual should consider that this is the exception with him and that the thing is all arranged to entice contributions for a godly purpose through hope of unearned profit.

49. *A layman may be admitted to Holy Communion even if he holds chiliastic views, if he agrees not to propagandize his views.*

Concerning your inquiry, my opinion is that it is certainly right to make a great differentiation between a pastor and a layman. The latter must only be asked if he would dispense with his chiliasm if he would be convinced otherwise from the Word of God and secondly if he would forego all propagation of his belief inside and outside the congregation. If he agrees to this and is a man free from fanaticism, simply trapped by error in his own naïveté, then he can be permitted to enter your congregation and to come to the Lord's Supper after it has been explained to him that you regard his chiliasm as a dangerous heresy but are willing to tolerate it in his case as a weakness.

50. *Walther did not favor liturgical innovations, but he was not entirely averse to some changes. He positively favored research in liturgical questions.*

As far as the drafting of new formularies is concerned, I have as little enthusiasm, I must confess, as my colleagues, with whom I have discussed this. The new church language has not yet emerged. We think that only that which is on hand from the good days should be published and only that awkward phrases should be polished up, obsolete words should be exchanged with words that are current and in use today, that which is offensive in appearance and form should be purged, etc. We will gladly accept a few samples of such newly edited excerpts in the original and in their new edition for *Lehre und Wehre.*

We would also like to warn you not to draw up formularies for ceremonial events which were introduced first in the period of Rationalism, e. g., for dedications of churches. In the Lutheran Church these take place not by "incantations," as in the Roman Church, but "by the Word of God" (equals sermon) "and prayer." It would be well if you would come here once and look about in the library to see if you can find something good for your collection.

51. *Less than two months before the organization of the Missouri Synod, Walther answered a letter from Biewend, later his colleague at Concordia Seminary. However, in 1847 Walther had not yet met Biewend. Walther addresses himself to Biewend's two questions. The first dealt with the formal organizing of a congregation. Walther urges that the congregation itself must be active in formulating the constitution. The second question dealt with the liturgy; Walther voiced his private disapproval of the liturgy which Wilhelm Loehe had dedicated to F. C. D. Wyneken. That section of the letter is omitted here. A final paragraph summarizes briefly Walther's reasons for a synodical organization.*

You wanted to hear my insignificant opinion of the procedures that you might observe concerning a congregational constitution and liturgy. These are my thoughts on the first point. The pastor has no power other than the power of the Word (1 Peter 5:3). Therefore, it is not within the scope of his office to force on the congregation any kind of a man-made constitution or to demand the acceptance of such a constitution as a condition for being a Christian congregation. As fully as we are united in regard to the goals we pursue, I nevertheless cannot share your view that you must first draw up a complete constitution and then make submission to it the condition for acceptance into membership.

When a pastor accepts a call, he ought not to consider the condition in which a congregation is, for the more miserable its condition the more it needs his ministry. He should first, through his ministry, upgrade it to the proper position. Only one thing ought to concern a pastor when he accepts a call, that he does not renounce his faith or agree to obligations contrary to God's Word. An orthodox pastor, therefore, should allow himself to be called only by such a congregation in which each member confesses: (a) that he holds the Scriptures of the Old and New Testaments to be God's Word; (b) that he holds the teaching of the divine Word to be true, as the church has set it forth (especially in the Small Catechism and the Augsburg Confession); (c) that he will devote himself to God-pleasing conduct and, where he has failed, will allow himself to be judged and corrected by God's Word; and finally, (d) that he will recognize him as his pastor and will render him spiritual obedience as long as he administers his office according to God's Word or until the Lord of the church calls him elsewhere through a regular call. Whoever accepts these four conditions, him I accept in God's name as a sheep [member] of the flock. When a congregation establishes a pastoral ministry according to these conditions, the essential basis for a Christian congregation, as I see it, is there.

Naturally it is the pastor's duty to see to it that the congregation learns to understand all the implications of these conditions, so that the mutual ties may not rest on appearances. For example, he should inform them that whoever accepts these conditions should profess the Lutheran doctrine of the sacraments, absolution, etc., as the only true teaching and should resign from all groups that reject this. Moreover, it should be pointed out beforehand that the congregation should not set a terminal date for the ministry of the person it has called, and the like. Now, if a congregation is organized in this way, I doubt that their first business is to set up a constitution, a rule book. Rather, I believe, circumstances themselves must dictate the necessity of a constitution; what is done then will be done in a way that is recognized as best. That which has stood the test of time is finally written down and is raised as a good ordinance to the church law, which one is expected to keep in the future. The pastor should introduce nothing that he has not first brought before the congregation for advice and approval. No constitution should be regarded as good, no matter how wholesome it may appear, if it will make the people timid and drive them out of the community of the Gospel. Therefore, no human ordinance may be unalterable. As soon as the constitution no longer fulfills its purpose, it must be possible to do away with it very quickly. The constitution must not rule over the congregation, but the congregation over the constitution. Rules should be as few as possible. Also, they must be easy to keep, suitable to the degree of knowledge and experience that the particular congregation has attained. It is painfully embarrassing, if it happens that a member of the congregation is to be excommunicated because the established constitution offends him or perhaps because he has a baseless fear of it, that he cannot be made rid of.

A pastor should act with the greatest wisdom lest he through ordinances arouse disorder or a disgust towards the church and her pure teachings. I believe for that matter that the opponents of the so-called Old Lutherans are not completely wrong in their recent charges that the latter place far too great an emphasis on the ordinances, usages, and ceremonies of our fathers.

There is no absolute order; it is always relative. A Lutheran must never lose sight of that if he does not wish to come to the traditional basis of the Roman Church. The established constitution must not appear to the congregation as a law that enslaves but rather as a record of its proven usages and at the same time also as something that is beneficial to it. It must come out of the life of, and be developed by, the congregation. It is not a dead precept, a dead letter, but rather a gain from existential experiences. If the pastor makes the rules and binds the congregation to them, then they are an imposed burden; but if they have been experienced and established for preservation in the future by the congregation, which the pastor himself has trained as legislator, then the congregation will struggle to protect them as they would their own treasure.

This is how I proceeded in my own congregation. We were without a written constitution for the first years. Only the above-mentioned conditions for the whole structure and the requirement for individual membership were administered orally and regulated by the congregation, until the congregation itself urged that because of the many circumstances which were occurring (about the rules they were adopting one after the other), something should be written down and signed by all voting members of the congregation, that is, all the men who were of age.

Forbearing any further argument, I commit these directions to your Christian judgment. It may be that you have expected something entirely different, above all something bigger and better from me. I give what I have.

. . . .

It is certainly true that by acting so independently there is great danger that many unlutheran things may creep into the congregations calling themselves Lutheran, and that because of so many external differences the congregations might easily become strange to one another. But just for this reason a really strong, vital, and active synodical union should be maintained and should be controlled in regard to the doctrine they hold, their government, liturgy, etc., by representation chosen from all the individual congregations, and because of conviction maintain external and internal unity.

52. The problem of having a constitution for a congregation and of its function seems to have been a rather persistent one during the early years of the Missouri Synod. Walther's evangelical approach and pastoral concern are evident in the following extract.

God's Word has given no explicit mandate on the necessary struc-

70

turing of parish affairs. How these are to be regulated we can indeed assuredly deduce from God's Word but only analogously (Titus 1:5) and from the general Biblical principle that everything be done to the glory of God, to the welfare of the church, and to the salvation of each individual (1 Cor. 12:7; 10:31; 14:40).

Luther is quite right when he says that every *order* which no longer serves for edification has already become *dis-order*. If love is to be the mistress of all *commandments*, all the more she is to be the mistress of all *orders*. As much as it grieves me, therefore, that your congregation does not wish to accommodate itself to an order that could be so salutary for it, if it were entered into in good faith (since the congregation can perceive neither the necessity of it nor its salutary benefits, or—God alone knows—it does not want to perceive this), so I must agree with you entirely when you maintain that you cannot leave your congregation and thus abandon it to destruction. You would indeed have the power to do so according to the *jus* [the *jus* of the *potestas jurisdictionis*, Apol. XXVII?], but since according to love we have no power "to destroy" but only "to improve" (2 Cor. 10:8; 13:10), you would never excuse such a use of power and rights, and thereby quiet your conscience, if the consequence was the loss of immortal souls. To be sure even in the church the axiom is applicable: *Fiat justitia, et pereat mundus;* but first, only *when* the issue is one of obedience to a clear commandment of the Lord, and second, *because* the *et pereat mundus* is impossible when the *fiat justitia* is practiced in the church, since the latter is precisely the medium, yes, the only medium, for the salvation of the world.

53. Walther commented on things indifferent, adiaphora, rites, and ceremonies in a letter to Sihler, when he asked him to revise a manuscript he (Sihler) had sent him. Christian liberty was a precious part of the Lutheran heritage to him.

Regarding the sermon on Christian liberty the questioning thought occurred to me that in it the so-called fourth degree about *traditiones humanae* or *ceremoniae* (human traditions or ceremonies), *ritus ecclesiastica* (ecclesiastical rites), adiaphora (things not commanded or forbidden), *res indifferentes* (things indifferent), etc., is not differentiated from the other degrees and emphasized enough. The Tenth Article of the Formula of Concord shows how important just this part of the doctrine of Christian liberty is for a Lutheran, on the one hand against the papacy, which wants to force ceremonies upon us, on the other hand against the Enthusiasts, who want to deprive us of them as

71

sinful. Therefore, the theme itself does not seem to be exhaustive. It is true, no interim from Rome is threatening us. However, on the other hand the fanatical sects and the Union try to deprive us of Christian liberty in *rebus adiaphoris* (in things indifferent). If this hint convinces you, I would advise you to revise your sermon once more. For that reason I am returning it to you.

54. *No one may claim conscience scruples if the conscience refuses instruction from God's Word. However, Walther does not want to violate consciences. The letter also shows Walther's concern for maintaining good relationships between congregations.*

1. Only such a person who can prove that he feels himself bound by a Word of God, and indeed is, can appeal to his conscience. Nevertheless, if then those with greater insight see that that individual errs, then his conscience must be spared, provided that one is not in a position to do away with his conscience scruples due to misunderstanding of the divine Word. However, if he cannot cite such Word of God by which he considers himself bound, and if in contrast one quotes in vain a Word that ought to satisfy his ostensibly troubled conscience, then he is not to be listened to when he uses his conscience as a pretext. According to God's Word at times even Christ's enemies think they are doing God a service (thus acting according to conscience) when they brutally persecute Christ's disciples (John 16:2-3). Moreover, according to the Word of God the Christian conscience makes this Word its supreme judge (John 8:20). Therefore, also when Saul acted according to God's Word and sacrificed, he had to hear the verdict: "Because thou has rejected the Word of the Lord, He hath also rejected thee from being king"! 1 Sam 15:23. Therefore Luther writes: "Even if you would urge your conscience, that will not help you. You are required first to allow your conscience and purpose *to be substantiated by the Scripture or to be instructed by it*. Because of that you have declined, and have stipulated publicly that you would not enter into a disputation on the basis of the Scripture but would stay with your accustomed usage as sanctioned by the Christian churches. With that you give enough evidence against yourself, that you have invented such a conscience and urge it as a pretence. For a really good conscience does and desires nothing better than that it might hear the instruction of the Scripture and discuss its matters on the basis of Scripture." . . .

2. . . . However, since it is nevertheless possible per se that such a person has an erring conscience in a specific case, your congregation is

acting correctly if indeed it does not grant the man a peaceful dismissal but leaves it to the conscience of the other congregation if it wants to accept him or not. Under different circumstances a Christian should not burden *someone else* with what *he* himself cannot do with a good conscience. The congregation has done everything for the man that a Christian congregation can do to bring him to the right understanding; therefore it is proper that it now saddles the sister congregation with the burden to investigate whether it must judge otherwise. This is only a testimony that it does not want to govern over anyone's conscience but wants to deal free and open before the world and Christendom.

55. *Walther, addressing himself to the situation of the church in the newly united German Empire, indicates under what conditions separation from the state church should take place. This letter is one of the very few in which Walther expresses himself about state churches.*

Furthermore, I am firmly convinced that if there are things in a church that militate against God's Word, to which the preacher must obligate himself, he not only has the duty to resign from his office but also, after all attempts at relief have been shattered, has the right and the freedom to declare a separation. . . . I cannot see even the slightest factor which would make separation wrong in such a case. For a state church is not a divine institution; in itself it is no more sacred than an American synod. While it may be true that a Christian and a Christian preacher should gladly belong to a state church as a lover of freedom and in Christian liberty even though it is very corrupt, as soon as it wants to rule over conscience, all piety toward it comes to an end.

What shall the laity do who are stuck in congregations where false teachers are pastors? Are they to participate in false worship, and languish, so that the peace between the state church and the false prophets in their midst may not be disturbed? In my view, no! They should insist on removal [of the pastor], and if this happens, then they should use the rights God has given them in Christ to elect a true servant of the Gospel, whether that be one who is already in office, and easily reached, or an independent one.

56. *Missouri Synod pastors frequently wrote C. F. W. Walther for advice on local situations. In the following letter Walther states his opinion on saloons and their influence on people's lives. Although C. F. W. Walther was firmly against saloons, he still advised pastors* *to approach this situation evangelically and to resort to church discipline only as the very last measure.*

I have no doubt that it is your solemn duty to take the lead against the operation of saloons, whether or not they are connected with a store. A saloonkeeper sins: against himself, since he hinders himself from living in "godliness and respect" (1 Timothy 2); against his own family, since a Christian household with family worship and Christian training is hardly possible in the saloonkeeper's life, which daily brings terrible annoyances to the family; against the customers, who are encouraged in their intemperance, dissoluteness, neglect of their families, etc.; against the whole city, which is demoralized by the saloons; and against the orthodox church and her pure doctrine, which is slandered because of the saloonkeepers. But where would I end up with this if I were to name everything that piles up more and more guilt on the saloonkeeper?

However, if the evil has really spread so that many consciences have become sluggish and dead against this abomination, then you certainly cannot immediately step in against it with church discipline. In your situation I would first of all draw up theses, and on the basis of these conduct a series of lectures in congregational meetings and permit everyone to ask questions, to offer objections, but also to confirm your presentation. Naturally it must happen in the greatest evangelical kindness, and above all you must attempt to reach the hearts of the saloonkeepers and their supporters and convince them that you are motivated only by love for their immortal souls in seeking to clarify the issue with God's Word.

One must neither use sharp or cutting language nor proceed with church discipline or excommunication until the milder approach has been used and thereby everything that might be done has been exhausted. The object must also be to convince the entire congregation and bring it around to the truth so that, if possible, no accomplice remains. However, if all is in vain as far as the saloonkeepers are concerned, then all that remains is to apply firm church discipline against them. If the congregation cannot be persuaded to put the ban into effect because some members object to it, the pastor *then* has no other alternative than to explain that those who recognize the evil of the saloon but insist on supporting it must be denied the Sacrament and be suspended from it. This is what has to happen, even though a few of the members grumble and even though there is a danger that the congregation may split. To look the other way here and to let oneself be

74

overcome by men in administering the Sacrament to such people living in sinful activities and to absolve them would be to partake in their sins and cast God's Word among the thorns.

57. Patient dealing with a congregation, faithful preaching of the Word, and joy in service should be a pastor's recourse when dealing with conditions in a congregation that he wants to change, Walther writes. Walther regarded dancing as evil, but a pastor who is new to a congregation must instruct the congregation.

As far as your question is concerned, my advice is that you by no means do anything direct against dancing right now. Such vanities cease by themselves when the members learn to know and to love Jesus. Until they know Him, preaching against such vanities is for them something that they do not yet understand. In this way they only develop a hatred for the Gospel. Such matters can be handled directly from the start when the whole congregation has come somewhat further in understanding, when the Word has already accomplished so much that the young people would do such things only with a troubled conscience, and if the pastor, whenever he deals with this matter more seriously, then has the congregation behind him. From the start one must show diligently how good one has it with Jesus, if one surrenders himself completely, and how vain are the joys of the world. They do not bring peace of heart but create wounds, which only leave behind that much greater grief. Don't worry yourself if you and your congregation cannot see eye to eye so soon. Preach the Word with vigorous courage, and then let God attend to it. In spite of the most disgusting abcesses of the soul, let nothing deprive you of your joy and love for your congregation.

58. The president of a congregation may not call a meeting of the congregation without the pastor's knowledge and consent. Such a situation ought be covered in the constitution, Walther writes.

You must tell the president [of the congregation] that you readily forgive him that he had set up a quasi-congregational meeting behind your back, so to speak, because you attribute it to his ignorance of his rights and duties. Also that from now on you cannot recognize any meeting as a congregational meeting, if it is arranged without your knowledge and consent, since you are the shepherd of the flock. If he does not accept this, then you must tell the congregation in his presence that this is a perversion of the divine order and an intrusion on your office; indeed it would, in part, rob you. In this instance you dare not yield a hairbreadth; otherwise, you will be laying the foundation for all kinds of disorder.

There ought to be a paragraph in the constitution that defines exactly the legality of congregational meetings that are held, namely, which are regular, and which would be valid extra meetings.

59. Walther favored private confession and cited the Lutheran Symbols in support of this institution. However, he respected the right of the congregation to make a change. Christian liberty had to be respected.

The following is my judgment and counsel to your question as how you should conduct yourself over against the two parties, one of which wishes you to cooperate in the discontinuation of the exclusive use of private confession, and the other desires you to hold to the old blessed institution of private confession.

First, as soon as opportunity presents itself, you will state that on your part you are for the retention of the exclusive use of private confession and absolution and that you would not concur if it were done away with, on the basis of the Augsburg Confession, Article XI. To be sure, you cannot condemn congregations that do not practice it without exceptions. However, since it is still in vogue in your congregation, it would cause you conscience scruples if you should let it drop.

At the same time you ought to explain Article X of the Formula of Concord and show from it: (1) that a pastor does not have the power to regulate things indifferent, that therefore you cannot use force here; (2) that the arrangement, change, and ending of such a church ordinance which is not commanded by God (see Augsburg Confession, Article XXV, toward end) is in the power of the whole local congregation, which alone can decide, of course, with you as their shepherd; (3) but that if a change is undertaken, this must be done, as the Formula of Concord says, "without frivolity and offense but in an orderly and appropriate way, as at any time may seem to be most profitable, beneficial, and salutary for good order, Christian discipline, evangelical decorum, and the edification of the church." . . .

Along with this you ought to admonish those who press for abolition to consider what they are doing, and whether in doing so they wish to observe the manner and way the Formula of Concord requires in such cases. . . .

It would be sad if also the few congregations that still have only private confession would abandon it. Therefore, the congregation should be informed of the excellent testimonies from the confessional writings and Luther's writings about the glory of this institution. But, of course, compelling will not do, for one simply cannot bind conscience to private confession, and Christian liberty dare not be disavowed for its sake.

VI. About the Lodge Question

Walther's attitude toward secret society was a pastoral one. He condemned secret societies or lodges, even as he condemned any organized group that did not promote the Gospel. Members of Lutheran congregations who were also lodge members should be instructed carefully. The pastor and congregation should not become impatient with them. Walther was conscious of the weaknesses of individuals, willing to recognize that they might have a weak faith, careful that none should be condemned out of hand. He did not want to see Christians become members of non-Christian burial societies. He was extremely scrupulous that no one be a partaker of another man's sins. Nevertheless, he urged an evangelical approach toward members who needed their understanding of the sinfulness of lodge membership increased, as he saw it.

His attitudes are revealed not only in one or two letters. They are expressly stated in a letter addressed to the council of a Lutheran church. We want to remember that these letters were written during the time that the "four points" were a matter of controversy within Lutheranism in America. One of these four points concerned membership in secret societies. Although Walther does not refer to this question of church polity among other Lutherans, we can be certain that he was acquainted with the controversy and the stand that other Lutheran synods were taking pro or con. Those circumstances, too, make these letters particulary pertinent.

60. Walther differed with others within the Missouri Synod in his approach to the "lodge question." However, he was anxious that this difference would not cause a controversy within the Synod. While opposing the secret societies, he did not want membership in a secret society to be judged as a mortal sin.

I must admit that I am somewhat hesitant about answering your dear letter. The reason is that my conviction on the question you lay before me deviates from that of very highly respected men in our Synod. If this had to do with a clear doctrine, it would not perturb me,

78

for then it could be said, "Plato is my friend, Socrates is my friend; but truth is a greater friend." But this is concerned not so much with a doctrine (for in the evaluation of secret societies we are perfectly one in accordance with God's Word) but with the practical application of doctrine in a concrete case. In this matter I proceed from this principle: If I cannot prove that he is a non-Christian, and if he is a man who confesses the same faith that I do, I do not exclude him either from the Lord's Supper or from membership in the congregation, even if he is stuck in various sins of ignorance and weakness. For if this latter is the reason for exclusion, whom will I accept? And if it is certain that Christ accepts someone, who am I to cast him out? If I make an exception in regard to secret societies, the principle that served as the basis for reception and admission of others disappears.

Of course, I would point out to such a candidate for membership in the congregation that his association is wrong, and I would try to persuade him to give it up. But if it became evident that I could not persuade him, I would nevertheless consider it my duty to receive him as a weak brother, but with a protest against his connection and with the explanation that I do it in the hope that he will investigate the matter once more after he has gotten a deeper understanding of God's Word. If a congregation has the stipulation in its constitution that no member of a secret society can be a member of the congregation, I consider that a mistake and very harmful, especially in areas where those societies predominate. Without doubt it locks the door to the Gospel for many souls who first come to a correct and clear understanding through the Gospel and then can be saved. What great patience Luther had with those who continued to drag their feet in papistical error and how carefully he tried to win them over. In the "Instruction for the Visitors" he expressed the wish that to those who could not be persuaded of the correctness of distribution of both kinds in the Lord's Supper, it be administered in one kind for a while, but that the *doctrine* be confessed and recognized and that there be no yielding to the *stiff-necked*. The whole discussion is of greatest importance in the present case and many others. . . .

I clearly see the danger which threatens us if we open the church to "lodge brothers." But it is better for love to accept the danger than to be unjust and deny to the children of God what is rightfully theirs through faith, yes, instead of compelling them to come in, to stand like an angel in front of the church to drive men back from its entrance with a fiery sword. I regard the matter as a severe temptation to us to cut off our influence on the masses because of a false conscience and thus either keep them in the sinful world or drive them to the sects. Would not such rigor easily lead to an Anabaptist-like conception of the necessary purity of the visible church?

In brief I still say that one should distinguish doctrine and life, justification and sanctification, and that in public and in private one should zealously oppose secret societies (although in such a manner that a mortal sin is not created out of what is a sin of weakness for many, and that the sin be judged not according to the deed but according to the person), but one should not throw out those who are stuck in them, who are not immediately convinced of their sinfulness, who cannot break away from them but otherwise demonstrate that they are repentant Christians. I would rather that you do not appeal to me in this matter, dear brother. Above all I do not want a practical question to be used by the devil to cast a firebrand into our midst.

61. Walther replied to a series of questions from a pastor of the Norwegian Synod. He expresses himself unequivocally as being opposed to membership in any society in which there are unbelievers and members of other denominations.

You ask, furthermore, "May members of a congregation hold membership with others who are not members of the congregation — Methodists or sectarians, even manifest children of the world and certainly nonconfessors of religion? May one join an organization in which members of another faith, or even unbelievers, are already members or are in charge of the situation?" My answer is, by no means! According to the Word of God every union with errorists or unbelievers is a horrible sin if that group concerns itself with matters that determine our relationship to God or deal with religion, faith, morals, life. What can be more unworthy of a Christian than to enter into a covenant with servants of the devil in order to battle against the devil at their side? What can be more contrary to love than for a Christian to place himself on a level with non-Christians and thus say to them that works done in unbelief are good works? No; here it must rather be said, "Come out from them, and be separate from them, says the Lord, and touch nothing unclean; then I will welcome you" (2 Cor. 6:17). To be associated with children of the world in matters connected with our earthly calling is an altogether different thing. For in such things the child of the world knows that the Christian does not at all intend to witness to him (1 Cor. 5:9-11).

62. Walther instructs a pastor to allow a lodge member to go to

Holy Communion at least for a while, because he is still weak in faith. He draws on Luther and finds an analogy with Luther's stand about the weak who wanted to receive Holy Communion under one kind. Those who give offense must be reconciled before they go to Holy Communion. The spirit of the Missouri Synod is one of integrity, humility, simplicity, and of regard for the church.

According to the small measure of my knowledge may the following serve as an answer to your inquiry.

Without doubt you are correct when you are convinced that we should not keep anyone from the Holy Supper, if he possibly is a true Christian and acknowledges with us one faith. For how can we deny the body and blood of Jesus Christ to one who is already a member of the spiritual body of Christ, even though he may still be weak, yes, very weak in knowledge, faith, and love. Indeed, God's Word commands us to receive the weak in faith, Romans 14:1, and to bear the infirmities of the weak, Romans 15:1. From that follows, however, of necessity that above all we ought not to refuse them the Sacrament, by which alone they become strong.

Therefore, if certain persons are for that reason still members of a secret society, as the one in which you described, because they are still very weak in understanding, they *cannot summarily* be refused the Holy Supper. Luther even at the beginning allowed those who made it a question of conscience about receiving the Holy Supper under both kinds to receive it under one kind.

However, Luther states expressly that this should be done only "for a time," until they came to understanding. However, "the stubborn," who wish "neither to learn nor to do" what is right he excludes from this. . . .

From this I conclude that if Luther were in our shoes he would also not deny the Supper to our poor Germans, who were so grievously neglected under Rationalism as the people once were under the papacy, even if they cannot yet perceive the sinfulness of their connection with that society. However, as he had patience with those only for a "time" and excluded those therefore who proved themselves stubborn and wished neither to learn nor to do what is right, so he would surely also observe these restrictions in our case.

. . . .

Therefore, my opinion is that for a while one allows people [to go to Communion] who are attached to secret societies and do not yet perceive what is sinful about them, if otherwise they show themselves to be Christians, insofar as one carries them because of their weakness. One cannot make any rules about how long this is to be done. All depends on the condition of the people. However, not only must they first be shown their fault, but one must also testify that this cannot continue forever, that this is being done with the hope that they would come to a better knowledge.

Perhaps one could argue that as long as they do not show themselves to be non-Christian, one dare not refuse them so that one does not deprive a child of God of his rights. However, this is refuted by what the Lord says: "If thou bring thy gift to the altar, and there rememberest that thy brother hath ought against thee; leave there thy gift before the altar, and go thy way; first be reconciled to thy brother, and then come and offer thy gift." Matt. 5:23-24.

Therefore as he who is not reconciled is not excommunicated because he is not a Christian, yet must reconcile himself *before* the offering and is to be *suspended* until that time, so also he who remains for years in an offensive organization in spite of all instruction without a doubt is to be suspended until he removes the offense and thus actually reconciles himself with the offended congregation. He is not to be suspended because of outward hindrances that require only a postponement of the use of the Holy Supper.

This question of secret societies has no precedent in ancient times; therefore we can decide and now deal only with analogies in agreement with the old church and its practice.

63. The following letter is given in full. In it Walther shows a pastoral concern for the weak brother and shows how this is compatible with the congregation's constitution.

According to the presentation of the case about which you desire my opinion, I think that the former member of your dear congregation, H. Piel, has not yet recognized the sinfulness of his lodge membership. From that he could easily become convinced that his exclusion from the congregation was a result of his little faith. However, it is impossible that little faith is a reason for excommunication, but solely deadly sin shown from the Word of God and brought to conviction, as the apostle does in 1 Corinthians 5:11, or manifest works of the flesh, as the same writes in Galatians 5:19-21. However, the congregation should first exhaust all means to bring the sinner to repentance according to Matt. 18:17; 2 Cor. 2:6; 2 Thess. 3:15; Titus 3:10.

Therefore I think that Mr. Piel should be admonished further, and he should be worked on, to strengthen his faith and to win him over from the sinfulness of his connection with the unbelievers in a secret, offensive, and vexing manner, which has the appearance of evil.

As long as Mr. Piel does not thereby show himself to be a despiser of God's Word, he cannot possibly be excommunicated, even if he cannot be convinced of the irreconcilableness of his membership in the lodge and in the church, partly because of a weakness in understanding, partly because of a lack of real earnestness and zeal.

It is true, your constitution requires that anyone who wants to be a member of your congregation may not be a member of a secret society. However, the breaking of a congregational constitution cannot result in excommunication, if thereby no sin is committed that according to God's Word results in excommunication. A lodge brother indeed suffers from that the loss of his membership and his share in the rights of a member of the congregation but not his rights as a Christian. Therefore, as long as he does not make himself liable to excommunication, Mr. Piel can lose only the right to vote in the congregation and the like, but not the rights of a Christian to be admitted to the Lord's Supper, to absolution, to be a sponsor.

Therefore, may the dear congregation have mercy on the poor, ignorant individual, who is weak in faith. May it continue to work on him, to turn him from the error of his ways. But this may not be done in such a way that he is provoked to opposition, but with that love that does not become weary and allows the erring one time to deliberate.

So be satisfied with this little. May God have mercy on the erring one and enlighten him, but protect the congregation that the offence given it may not harm it but exercise it in love.

64. *This letter does not bear directly on the lodge question. However, it shows Walther's opposition to sharing even cemeteries and buildings with non-Lutherans.*

I have no doubt that buying a cemetery and allowing also the heterodox to conduct their mostly godless funeral services there would conflict with the divine command: "Not to participate in another man's sins." In funeral sermons especially God's Word, more than usually, is shamefully distorted, misused, and souls are misled into false security.

Momentarily I simply do not have the time to furnish you with suitable testimony. Now then, try once to tackle the case alone with a Bible verse. True, without a doubt you will have to proceed gently, since the point is ticklish and for a dull conscience not so sensitive, and yet the fact must stand not to give aid to something evil. If the case is not settled immediately, the leaven will penetrate, if only it is worked into the dough. . . .

. . . .

[P. S.] It is self-evident where an agreement of various faiths about the use of a building, a property, etc., includes a joint purchase, the contract will have to stand, although it should not have been made, unless needed, and later the orthodox were allowed to use it with them. Then the heterodox would be allowing its use and not the other way around.

VII. About Personal Sorrows and Joys

Personal joys and sorrows, especially the latter, were occasions for letters by Walther to his children and friends. In these letters he appears as a pastor applying spiritual comfort, administered to each person according to his own needs. Walther makes liberal applications of the Gospel promises, finding in them the sources of comfort and strength. He looks beyond the present to the future. His eschatological references pervade his own theology of hope. The frequent quotations from and references to the Scriptures are accompanied in some instances by recitations from the hymnody of the church, with which Walther had a thorough acquaintance. Several of the letters translated in this section bring out some of Walther's personal characteristics — tenderness, consideration for others, seriousness, flashes of humor, and the like. Their value as messages to today's church lies in the timelessness of the Gospel assurance.

65. Walther's birthday greetings to Ferdinand encourage him in his work as pastor and beg him to rely on God. Success is in God's hands and is to be measured by God's criterion.

This last year of your life was, without a doubt, the most decisive one for you. In it God called you into the high and blessed office of the Gospel. And because God does nothing in time that He has not already decided in eternity, there can be no doubt that He also chose you already in eternity as His servant in His church. So God spoke to Jeremiah: "Before I formed thee in the belly, I knew thee; and before thou camest forth out of the womb, I sanctified thee, and I ordained thee a prophet unto the nations" Jeremiah 1:5. We poor sinners can easily get the idea: Oh, how can we compare ourselves to such a great prophet? That is easy enough to believe that God had chosen a Jeremiah already in eternity, but how can we believe that God thought of us already in eternity and designated us as His servants? But that is foolish rationalizing. With God there is no respect for persons. God has created and redeemed us, so also it is not too much for Him to think of us already in eternity and to allot to us our destiny.

Therefore, on your birthday consider how wonderfully, how benevolently, how wisely God has led you up to now. Even if the congregation allotted to you is small, the ministry you occupy is great, important, and blessed. And if you in your ministry were to bring only one soul on the right way, or keep it on it, then something inexpressibly great would be accomplished through you. The church father Lactantius wrote: . . . "I will believe that I have lived enough and fulfilled the duty of a man, if my work has freed a few men from errors and has shown them the heavenly way."

66. *Walther thanks his nephew (and future son-in-law) for a birthday gift, congratulates him on passing his final examination as a candidate for the holy ministry, and tells him how important it is for him to preach the Gospel. The Gospel must be the center of his ministry.*

I must write to you at least a few lines, first, in order to express my heartfelt thanks both for your gracious congratulations and for the precious gift of the history by von Ranke, which because of the poverty of your purse and the riches of your love overwhelmed me. As far as the latter is concerned, I am almost inclined to be angry with you, because you have shamed me with it. You should not give to me, but I, your uncle, should give gifts to you. Still I am a debtor to so many hearts that I might as well remain also a debtor to you. May God repay you for your love!

It was a great joy for me that you passed the examination so well. Because your previous studies in the last year had not entirely prepared you for an American theological examination, I was worried that the results, through my fault, could discourage you somewhat. But I am so much happier that this was not the case. May God now give you real joy in carrying out your office. I suspect your post is indeed not completely according to your wishes but, in any case, according to your need. If later you will get a congregation that you first must cultivate, not only to water it, but even plant it, you will have already gathered important experience and attained skill in preaching through God's help. Do not forget what the Augsburg Confession says in Article XXVI: "The doctrine of grace and justification by faith is the principal part of the Gospel and it is necessary for it to stand out greatly and be prominent in the church." The Law must be taught in all its severity; especially must be shown its spiritual sense,

86

its unfulfillable demands, its sure curse on all workrighteousness —
however, only to prepare and enable souls to hear and receive the Gospel of grace and righteousness of faith. Along with this must go the sweet, full, clear, loud Gospel of Christ, which proclaims to all who are in uncertainty, sorrow, difficulty, doubt, and danger about their salvation, nothing but grace without works of the Law, righteousness, merit, or quality. That must not only *extare*, exist, in the church, but also *eminere*, be prominent, above all as the most important thing, indeed as the true heart and core of every sermon. That and nothing else creates truly happy, willing for every good, loving, humble, kind, zealous, true Christians. If this fails or if it does not become prominent, then a congregation receives no true joy in Christ, in their Christianity, in their church, and it will not take root or become established, but it will remain stuck in a powerless legalism.

If one sees the people's great weaknesses, faults, marks of insincerity, and if one learns of outbreaks of open carnality, then one is tempted to keep for himself the precious pearl of the message of grace. But that is false. Nothing but this message can help miserable, sick, dead, ruined mankind out of his ruin. Note that and cry out real loudly: "Let us be reconciled with God! Come, everything is ready! Come, there still is room! Ho, everyone that thirsteth, come ye to the waters, and he that hath no money; come ye, buy, and eat; yea, come, buy wine and milk without money and without price." If you do that, you will have much more joy in your ministry. Then you will know that you will not go astray, that you will preach the truth, and that even if many a one is still not won over through it, he might still seize in death the anchor you held out to him.

67. Walther believed that peace with compromise would be a happy solution of the Civil War. Especially the Lutherans should know that God calls peacemakers "blessed."

Now, since the Confederates have renewed the invasion in the eastern states, we think of you often not without worry. Still we hope that if at some time they come even to Philadelphia, you would escape with a wholesome terror. I say "with a wholesome," because without a doubt there are still very many in the North who are not for peace by compromise, because they themselves have experienced nothing of the terror of war. . . . Oh, that the Christians, and above all the Lutherans, would take to heart the Word of the Lord: "Blessed are the peacemakers" (οἱ εἰρηνοποιοί = makers of peace), "for they shall be called the children of God" (Matthew 5 [v. 9]). But one is deaf to that. . . .

68. *Walther's son and namesake had spiritual difficulties in the early years of his ministry. Walther addresses him with a warm paternal and pastoral heart. Noteworthy in this letter, too, is the glimpse into Wyneken's prayer practices. Walther also indicates that he had troubles of his own.*

. . . Although this last letter is still accompanied with the complaint that despair grips you in many hours, that your heart seems almost to want to break, I hope that our faithful God will not allow you to go under in your need. For, after all, He has created you, dearly redeemed you by the blood of His Son, and in baptism has accepted you as His child and heir. Therefore He cannot forsake you nor neglect you. For all that, He has announced to all sinners by the prophet Isaiah, 1:18: "Though your sins be as scarlet, they shall be white as snow; though they be red like crimson, they shall be as wool." In the final analysis God has worked in you the will not to serve sin; therefore He will also not permit the little spark of your faith to be extinguished, and eventually He will fan it into a bright flame with the breath of His mouth through the Word.

> And if woe lasts throughout the night
> And fills the day with sorrow,
> My heart despairs not of His might
> Nor grieves until the morrow.

"They that wait upon the Lord shall renew their strength; they shall mount up with wings as eagles; they shall run and not be weary; and they shall walk and not faint." Isaiah 40 [v. 31]

You write that when you preach, it is as if you are showing others the way to heaven and you yourself were being lost; your preaching is a mere mouthing. However, that is only the voice of the flesh and of the evil foe, who would like to thrust you into despair. Only preach Christ confidently and boast of His grace. After all, that is the doctrine the Lord commanded His disciples to preach. Such preaching is therefore the best thing that you can perform in your present calling. You yourself should believe in that which you preach; then your preaching will help not only your hearers but also yourself. For that is the way it should be. After all, the apostle writes: "Take heed unto thyself, and unto the doctrine; continue in them: for in doing this *thou shalt save both thyself* and them that hear thee" 1 Tim. 4:16. Also you should not think, when you feel yourself to be dead and unbelieving while you are preaching, that therefore your preaching is dead mouthing. Oh, no. God's Word is and remains living and powerful (Hebrews 4:12). Applying this to yourself, you must consider that faith is not an emotion but a trust in the word of promise, a sure confidence in what one *hopes,* and does not doubt in that which one does not *see* (Hebrews 11:1) and therefore does not experience.

. . . .

O my dear Ferdinand, learn only to trust your Savior. He is friendly and gracious. Whoever comes to Him, He will not cast out. Let what is written in the Epistle for the Fourth Sunday in Advent be said to you: "Rejoice in the Lord always; and again I say, Rejoice" Phil. 4:4. Open your heart to the joy of Christmas, for it proclaims a joy "which shall be to all people," among whom you also belong. Say in the words of the hymn:

Hence all fear and sadness!
For the Lord of gladness,
Jesus enters in.

Not long ago I wrote to dear Wyneken that you were beset with grave spiritual distress, and I asked him to include you in his petitions. Yesterday I received a letter from him, in which he wrote among other things: "I have put your dear Ferdinand on the list of those for whom I pray *daily,* immediately after his father. When he is again out of the fire, I would like to know about it. I would then put him again in the *general* list, and another would then be found whom I would substitute for him. The Lord who beholds the distressed will also look at him in grace and will make something substantial out of him, to the glory of His name, which cannot happen without severe trial." See, you have another good advocate besides us. We will not cease to cry to God for you and say; "We will not let Thee go, except Thou bless us" (cf. Genesis 32:26). Therefore wait upon the Lord!

Here we too have enough trouble, as you can imagine. Because I must always wield the pen, I am especially vulnerable when a storm arises. However, I will not allow the devil to triumph over me. I know that the devil raves and rages against us just because we are in his way. Even if he would always find a Judas among Christ's disciples, that will not help him but will only harm him and help us. Even if the world and the false church should laugh at us, "he who laughs last laughs best."

89

69. *Another letter to his son Ferdinand to cheer him up. Walther was fond of quoting from the hymnological treasures of the church, as this and other letters demonstrate.*

. . . I am sorry that the spirit of melancholy and despair has not yet left you. Nevertheless, remember that *this* spirit does not come from God, for we sing of the Holy Spirit in that hymn: "Enter, etc." Oh then, bid melancholy be gone! Spoil the devil's game that he seeks to play with you — in which he would make everything seem so gloomy. Although your position is a burden to you, God has hitherto helped you through all difficulties. Therefore set about defiantly to declare to the devil and to the world:

> The world against me rages, Its fury I disdain;
> Though bitter war it wages, Its work is all in vain.
> My heart from care is free, No trouble troubles me.
> Misfortune now is play, And night is bright as day.

Hallelujah! Many things continuously afflict me, but I will not be ensnared by them. That one gives way to worry does not detract a bit from the misery but rather only aggravates it. Solomon says, Prov. 15:15, "A cheerful heart has a continual feast."

70. *Walther as father demonstrates his pastoral concern for his daughter Magdalene. In a birthday letter to her he brings her comfort and encouragement. She had married her cousin, the Rev. Stephan Keyl. Walther's piety, verging on Pietism, is evident throughout the letter.*

Remembering that at the end of this week it is your 31st birthday, I cannot help offering you my heartfelt, fatherly good wishes. Oh, may this new year of your life bring you anew grace, happiness, and blessing! To you and yours, bodily health, to you personally, peace and cheerfulness, forgiveness of sins, protection and shelter against evil, rich comfort in all the troubles of this life. When it seems as though darkness is enveloping you, may the hope arise that things will soon be better, and the sun will shine again after the rain. In all your ways may God's Word be your rod and staff and give you counsel when you have no counsel of your own! If God puts a burden on you, may He be your strength and help you carry it. If crosses come, may He give you patience and resignation. If temptations come, may He let them soon pass and help you fight bravely to a joyful victory.

May He keep safely your dear husband and your precious children and let them always be a source of refreshment to you.

Do not take it amiss when also you must experience some of the troublesomeness of this life both inwardly and outwardly. This is the lot of all children of God. Since God does not want to damn us with the world but wants us to be saved, He cannot deal with us otherwise. If things always go well with us, we forget God only too easily, and we stop praying diligently and ardently to call on Him.

But if God sends us difficulty from which men cannot rescue us, He thereby compels us to seek refuge in Him. Therefore, do not think: this one or that one has it so much better; why does God let me experience so much unrest, fear, and anxiety? Ah, God cannot mean it better for us than when He often leads us into the dear school of the cross!

. . . .

Also, do not forget the innumerable blessings God has given you up to now and still gives you daily. How many there are whose entire life is a true hell! Always sickness, always poverty, always shame and contempt, and no true friend at their side, no loving and sympathetic relatives, no God and Savior, no star of hope! How fortunate you are in comparison! . . .

And now my sincerely beloved daughter, be commended to our faithful God. He, who created you, redeemed you at great cost, sanctified you already in Holy Baptism, who has brought you to the knowledge of His Son, your Savior, who up to now has wonderfully and graciously governed and guided you, will be your God and Father in the future and will take you under the wings of His grace as a hen gathers her chickens under her.

71. *Walther was the pastor of the pastors of the Missouri Synod. This letter to Barth is a beautiful testimony of his genuine pastoral concern. Barth had just lost his four children, all in one week. In a loving and gentle way Walther compares Barth with Job.*

First, God's comfort!

After reading your dear letter of the 8th of this month, which I received today with its heartrending news, I am deeply moved, and I must tear myself away from everything else, no matter how urgent, to assure you that you have brothers who weep and lament with you. My first reaction was to cry out with Isaiah: "Truly, Thou art a God who hidest Thyself." Yet, I was reminded at the same time that God has lifted His hiddenness in His Word. For God tells us quite plainly that it is a sign how much He *loves* His *children* when He disciplines them, not how angry He is with them. The writer of the Epistle to the

Hebrews writes: "'The Lord disciplines him whom He *loves*, and chastises every son whom He receives.' It is for discipline that you have to endure. God is treating you as sons; for what son is there whom his father does not discipline? If you are left without discipline, in which all have participated, then you are illegitimate children and not sons."

As your friend and brother, I comfort you with that; comfort yourself with that, and raise yourself up! After all, you believe in the Lord Jesus; you are also God's child. How *much* God must love you therefore, since He has buffeted you so severely. What *glory* above must God have prepared for you, since He Himself says: "May those who sow in tears reap with shouts of joy! He that goes forth weeping, bearing the seed for sowing, shall come home with shouts of joy, bringing his sheaves with him." . . .

In your great sorrow, by which God has made you conformable with the great saint [Job], go "into the sanctuary of God," i. e., the Holy Scriptures, then you and your dear wife too, like Asaph, will overcome all temptations. To be sure, Satan will also make his appearance and shoot his fiery darts into your heart, but extinguish them with the shield of faith. "Prayer, meditation, tribulation make a theologian." It is very evident that God wants to make a real theologian out of you, therefore He matriculates you in the graduate school of His kingdom, the school of severe tribulations.

I am amazed to see in your letter how heroic God made you. Oh, may God continue to strengthen you and by you make Satan a laughing stock and scandal! It may well be that a flood of tears will flow even more abundantly from your eyes and those of your wife *after* your first victorious struggle with doubt, yes with despair. But weep! You would have no parental love if you could restrain your tears, of which the Son of God was not ashamed at the grave of Lazarus. However, I hope that in time your tears will flow less copiously and will often change over into tears of joy for the glory in which you know all your dearly beloved children to be. I cannot tell you how lovely the picture was for me which you drew in your first letter of your now sainted child. Oh, how much joy you have *lost*, which you had before this in your sweet olive shoot! As often as you think about this, lift your tear-filled eyes to the blessed Paradise and revel in this, how much your little sweetheart won by way of contrast. Oh, why do we not wish to dry our tears readily? Who knows how soon we too must close our eyes here, so that we can open them there, where we shall see with amazement the loved ones who have gone before us, embrace them, and then cultivate an eternal fellowship with them, which no woe can disturb and no death can end.

72. *Walther's daughter was very lonely while her husband was on a trip to Europe. Walther himself wrote a letter of encouragement to her and in this letter, too, shows himself a compassionate and loving parent. He recalls his own personal experience to encourage Magdalene.*

You write that you think of yourself as a widow. This I will readily grant you. It is difficult for a woman to stay at home alone for a long time with her small children. But first you must remember that you have a husband who is working for the kingdom of God. For that reason he forsakes wife and children and undertakes a dangerous journey. In the second place you have the joyful prospect of seeing him again soon and hugging him.

By the goodness of God we, your parents, are still together. But we are like a vine from which the leaves and grapes have been stripped; we have no longer hope that there will be new branches and grapes on our vine. We are happy with our lot, since our children are well provided for; and what is more important, that they know how to walk in the ways of the Lord. Reconcile yourself with the lot, which the good hand of your heavenly Father has given you. We really cannot order from God as good a life as He Himself in His counsel of love has allotted us. Only in eternity shall we perceive how graciously God has led us. There we will thank God ardently for what we here in our shortsightedness sighed and wept over. Let us be diligent in prayer. Prayer is the best key to God's gifts, which we need, the safest ladder by which we can climb out of the grave of all distress, all trouble, and all sorrow.

73. *Conflicts and controversies within the church are fiery trials. Pastors have glorious promises, Walther writes, on which they can rely. They can count themselves "blessed" and should be "joyful, joyful, joyful in hope."*

Finally, do not allow the fiery trial, which you are encountering, to estrange you, inasmuch as you are being tried as if you were experiencing something rare (1 Peter 4:12). In this crucible all must [be tried], whom God will not permit to become reprehensible in the ministry and to become lost.

According to Luther "to preach God's Word is nothing else than to array all the raging and ranting of all hell and the devil, after that all of his holy ones, the world, and all his might in the world." . . . Moreover, God would not give such glowing promises to the office of preaching, as in Daniel 12:3, if it were not a thousand times more difficult to be a pastor than to be only a Christian.

Strengthen yourself, therefore, together with your faithful spouse with the "blessed" which the Lord repeats ten times in Matthew 5. In their place world and flesh would put a tenfold "woe." Learn the "leaping" about which Christ speaks, Luke 6:23, which no "jumping Methodist" can do, only an evangelical Lutheran. Give the devil grief by laughing at his raging and ranting. After all, it is only the barking, snarling, and the showing of teeth of a chained dog.

In short be joyful, joyful, joyful in hope. You have a reason for that, for you are a Christian, thus a prophet, priest, and king. What more do you want?!

74. Thanks for a bottle of cherry wine in a spirit of good humor.

After I have carefully sampled your cherry wine, I can hardly recover from my astonishment that something so delicious grows in your Will County, which, as you know, lies closer to the North Pole than our St. Louis County, not even to mention Saxony, where, of course, since my enforced flight, nothing, not even the famed Saxon stocking wine, turns out well. Your cherry wine has only one drawback, namely, the remarkable way that the larger the glass is that one fills with it, the more critically empty the bottle becomes. It is not like the barometer, which although it also often falls, yet after waiting a day it often rises again. I have observed it closely and have clearly noticed that your bottle of cherry wine has never risen again on the following day. I wonder if perhaps that is only due to the local climate? Please, share with me soon your observation of the weather in this matter, for if the opposite holds true in Will County, I think I will retire and move to that blessed county.

But all joking aside! A thousand thanks for your friendly thoughts about your old, unworthy friend. As much as that delicious drink has refreshed me (I speak the truth and do not flatter my benefactor) and, God willing, will still refresh me, yet this proof of your love has refreshed me even more. I sincerely ask you only one thing: that you do not suspect my gratitude is based on the proverb: *"Gratiarum actio ad plus dandum imitatio."* If you carry out your decision to send me more in the fall, if I like it, you would plunge me into despair, so that in order not to appear impudent, I would have to write to you [that] your nectar was a lye; and that would be an infamous lie.

Appendix: References

In each instance the writer of the letter is C. F. W. Walther. The asterisk (*) indicates that the letter is in the C. F. W. Walther files at Concordia Historical Institute, St. Louis, Mo., and that it was transcribed by Prof. Werner Karl Wadewitz.

Briefe is the abbreviation used for L. Fuerbringer, editor, *Briefe von C. F. W. Walther an seine Freunde, Synodalgenossen und Familienglieder* (2 vols.; St. Louis: Concordia Publishing House, 1915–16).

1. To the Rev. Wilhelm Sihler, Ph. D., Pomeroy, Ohio, 2 January 1845. *Briefe,* I, 6–12. Translation by the Rev. Marcus Berndt.

2. Translation by Carl S. Meyer, "Walther's Letter from Zurich: A Defense of Missouri's Unity and Confessionalism," 16 June 1860, *Concordia Theological Monthly,* XXXII (October 1961), 650–55.

3. To Mr. Eggen, Berlin, Prussia, 29 August 1862. *Briefe,* I, 180–83. Translation by Dr. Robert Kolb.

4. To the Rev. Wilhelm Sihler, Ph. D., Fort Wayne, Indiana, 22 January 1876.* Translation by Carl S. Meyer.

5. To Mr. Gustav Stegner, location undetermined, 1 October 1863.* Translation by Dr. Robert Kolb.

6. To the Rev. Henry C. Schwan, Cleveland, Ohio, 29 June 1867. *Briefe,* II, 101. Translation by the Rev. John Pohanka.

7. To the Rev. Henry C. Schwan, Cleveland, Ohio, 26 April 1870. *Briefe,* II, 191. Translation by the Rev. John Pohanka.

8. To the Rev. Fr. Brunn, Steeden, Nassau, spring 1866. *Briefe,* II, 35–36. Translation by the Rev. John Pohanka.

9. To the Rev. Fr. Brunn, Steeden, Nassau, 4 January 1868. *Briefe,* II, 122. Translation by the Rev. John Pohanka.

10. To the Rev. Fr. Brunn, Steeden, Nassau, 21 May 1870. *Briefe,* II, 194. Translation by the Rev. John Pohanka.

11. To the Rev. Wilhelm Loehe, Neuendettelsau, Bavaria, 5 June 1852.* Translation by Prof. Herbert J. A. Bouman.

12. To the Messrs. H. Reif, W. Albrecht, etc., Detroit, Mich., 16 May 1876.* Translation by Carl S. Meyer.

13. To Mr. Quabius, location not given, 20 September 1870.* Translation by Carl S. Meyer.

14. To the Rev. Ottomar Fuerbringer, Frankenmuth, Michigan, 22 March 1870. *Briefe*, II, 186. Translation by Mr. Michael Moore.

15. To the Rev. Frederick Lochner, Milwaukee, Wisconsin, 1 February 187? *(sic)*. *Briefe*, II, 191–92. Translation by Mr. Michael Moore.

16. To "Madam," location not given, 10 May 1862.* Translation by Dr. Robert Kolb.

17. To the Rev. Adam Ernst, Elmira, Ontario, Canada, 10 April 1868. *Briefe*, II, 125–26. Translation by Mr. Michael Moore.

18. To the Rev. Henry C. Schwan, Cleveland, Ohio, 17 December 1869. *Briefe*, II, 166. Translation by Mr. Michael Moore.

19. To the Rev. J. F. Buenger, St. Louis, 5 December 1865.* Translation by Dr. Robert Kolb.

20. To the pastors of the Missouri Synod, 12 January 1875.* Also in *Zeuge und Anzeiger*, V, 50 (14 May 1905), 391–92. Translation by the Rev. John Pohanka.

21. To the Rev. F. W. T. Steimle, Brooklyn, New York, 25 January 1861.* Translation by Dr. Robert Kolb.

22. To the Rev. J. A. Ottesen, Utica, Wisconsin, 9 January 1860. *Briefe*, I, 129–30. Translation by Dr. L. Blankenbuehler.

23. To the Rev. Jacob Stirewalt, New Market, Shenandoah County, Virginia, 19 February 1859.* Translation by Dr. Edward H. Schroeder.

24. To the Rev. Stephan Keyl, Philadelphia, Pa., 29 July 1866, *Briefe*, II, 129–30. Translation by Mr. Michael Moore.

25. To the Rev. U. V. Koren (?), Decorah, Iowa, 9 March 1870. Translation by Dr. Paul E. Kretzmann, *The Clergy Bulletin*, XII (February and March 1953), 80.

26. To the Rev. Fr. Brunn, Steeden, Nassau, 5 December 1873.* Translation by the Rev. Carl F. Baase.

27. To the Rev. Ulrich V. Koren, Decorah, Iowa, 19 February 1880.* Translation by Carl S. Meyer.

28. To the Rev. Ferdinand Walther, Brunswick, Mo., 9 September 1871. Chr. W. Hochstetter, "Erinnerungen an Dr. C. F. W. Walther," *Zeuge und Anzeiger*, V (2 April 1905), 346–47. Translation by Mr. Michael Moore.

29. To the Rev. John Walther, Wyandotte, Mich., 8 September 1863. *Briefe*, I, 191–92. Translation by Carl S. Meyer.

30. To the Rev. H. Engelbrecht, Chicago, Ill., 1 September 1873.* Translation by the Rev. Edward N. Bartell.

31. To the Rev. Th. Ruhland, Buffalo, New York, 8 May 1867. *Briefe*, II, 95–97. Translation by Mr. Michael Moore.

32. To the Rev. J. Fackler, Lyons, Iowa, 20 February 1879.* Translation by Carl S. Meyer.

33. To the Rev. J. Timothy Steimke in Texas, 7 January 1880.* Translation by the Rev. A. W. Reese.

34. To "My dear Reverend Sir," 19 March 1870.* Translation by Carl S. Meyer.

35. To "Honorable Friend and Brother," 26 September 1867. Translation by Dr. Paul E. Kretzmann, *The Clergy Bulletin*, XII (February and March 1953), 81–82.

36. To an unknown pastor, 18 January 1829 *(sic* for 1849).* Translation by Carl S. Meyer.

37. To the Rev. C. A. Mennicke, Rock Island, Illinois, 11 February 1856.* Translation by Prof. Herbert J. A. Bouman.

38. To the Rev. J. C. W. Lindemann, Cleveland, Ohio, 4 June 1864. *Briefe*, I, 203 – 4. Translation by Prof. William M. Ewald.

39. To Director J. C. W. Lindemann, Addison, Illinois, 27 September 1866. *Briefe*, II, 55 – 56. Translation by Prof. William M. Ewald. The conclusion of this letter reads: "The Lord be with you and preserve you in your hitherto sincere community of faith in which you have been with your upright co-workers and – in spite of some hay and stubble – with your least brother, C. F. W. Walther."

40. To the Rev. J. A. Ottesen, Koshkonong, Wisconsin, 29 December 1858. *Briefe*, I, 115 – 19. Translation by Dr. L. Blankenbuehler.

41. To "Reverend Sir," location unknown, 19 March 1870.* Translation by Carl S. Meyer.

42. To the Rev. C. A. Mennicke, Rock Island, Illinois, 16 September 1861.* Translation by Dr. Robert Kolb.

43. To the Rev. A. F. Hoppe, New Orleans, Louisiana, 4 January 1865. *Briefe*, I, 206. Translation by Mr. Michael Moore.

44. To "Dear Brother," location not known, 21 February 1883.* Translation by the Rev. B. F. Behrends.

45. To "Dear Brother in the Lord," location not known, 16 November 1865.* Translation by Carl S. Meyer.

46. To the Rev. A. G. Schieferdecker, Altenburg, Missouri, 11 February 1847.* Translation by Carl S. Meyer.

47. To "My dear Pastor," location not known, 4 December 1869.* Translation by the Rev. A. M. Bickel.

48. To the Rev. H. Fick, Boston, Mass., 26 November 1872.* Translation by the Rev. A. M. Bickel.

49. To the Rev. C. A. Mennicke, Rock Island, Illinois, 29 May 1861.* Translation by Dr. Robert Kolb.

50. To the Rev. F. Lochner, Springfield, Illinois, 4 February 1879.* Translation by Carl S. Meyer.

51. To the Rev. Adolph Biewend, Georgetown (Washington D. C.), 10 March 1847.* Translation by Mr. William H. Winkler.

52. Addressee unknown, located in Milwaukee, Wisconsin, 5 February 1856.* Translation by Dr. Edward H. Schroeder.

53. To Dr. Wilhelm Sihler, Fort Wayne, Indiana, 14 November 1882.* Translation by the Rev. Ronald W. Goetsch.

54. To the Rev. J. H. Werfelmann, Milwaukee, Wisconsin, 2 January 1874.* Translation by Carl S. Meyer.

55. To the Rev. Fr. Brunn, Steeden, Nassau, 5 December 1873.* Translation by the Rev. Carl F. Baase.

56. To the Rev. August Senne, Buffalo, New York, 7 July 1882.* Translation by the Rev. B. F. Behrends.

57. To the Rev. John Walther, Wyandotte, Michigan, 8 September 1863. *Briefe*, I, 192. Translation by Mr. Michael Moore.

58. To the Rev. John Walther, Wyandotte, Michigan, 9 June 1866. *Briefe*, II, 44 – 45. Translation by Mr. Michael Moore.

59. To the Rev. W. Linsenmann, Fischerville, Ontario, 28 June 1881.* Translation by the Rev. Paul Prokopy.

60. To the Rev. J. G. Kuechle, Columbus, Indiana, 16 August 1864.* The letter does not name the addressee. The identification is made on the basis of a letter from the

Rev. J. G. Kuechle to the Rev. H. C. Schwan, 23 July 1890.* Translation by Dr. Robert Kolb. We are indebted to Dr. Kolb and Dr. Aug. R. Suelflow for identifying the addressee. A mimeographed copy of another translation of this letter erroneously identifies the addressee as the Rev. F. Wyneken.

61. To the Rev. J. A. Ottesen, Koshkonong, Wisconsin, 5 January 1866. *Briefe,* II, 8–9. The translation is from Carl S. Meyer, ed., *Letters of C. F. W. Walther: A Selection* (Philadelphia: Fortress Press, 1969), pp. 107–8.

62. To the Rev. A. Rohrlach, Reedsburg, Wisconsin, 13 January 1868.* Translation by Carl S. Meyer.

63. To the church council of the Lutheran Church in Vincennes, Indiana, 15 July 1870.* Translation by Carl S. Meyer.

64. To Director J. C. W. Lindemann, Addison, Illinois, 12 January 1873.* Translation by the Rev. Paul J. Affeldt.

65. To the Rev. Ferdinand Walther, Brunswick, Mo., 21 February 1870. *Zeuge und Anzeiger,* V (26 March 1905), 336–37. Translation by Mr. Michael Moore.

66. To Stephan Keyl, Baltimore, Maryland, 15 March 1862. *Briefe,* I, 175–76. Translation by Mr. Michael Moore.

67. To the Rev. Stephan and Mrs. Keyl, Philadelphia, Pa., 29 July 1864. *Briefe,* I, 205. Translation by Mr. Michael Moore.

68. To the Rev. Ferdinand Walther, Brunswick, Mo., 13 December 1871.* Translation by Carl S. Meyer. A portion of this letter is found also in Chr. W. Hochstetter, "Erinnerungen an Dr. C. F. W. Walther," *Zeuge und Anzeiger,* V, 45 (9 April 1905), 352–53.

69. To the Rev. Ferdinand Walther, Brunswick, Mo., 1 June 1872.* Translation by the Rev. C. L. Bliss.

70. To his daughter Magdalena, wife of the Rev. Stephan Keyl, New York, N. Y., 17 November 1873.* Translation by the Rev. Edward N. Bartell.

71. To the Rev. G. A. Barth, Pella, Wisconsin, 11 June 1880.* Translation by Carl S. Meyer.

72. To his daughter Magdalena, wife of the Rev. Stephan Keyl, New York, N. Y., 19 March 1873.* Translation by the Rev. Emil Becker.

73. To "Reverend Sir," location unknown, 19 March 1870.* Translation by Carl S. Meyer.

74. To the Rev. E. A. Brauer, Crete, Illinois, 12 September 1880.* Translation by the Rev. Walter C. Meyer.

PHOTO ALBUM

CARL FERDINAND WILHELM WALTHER
(Concordia Historical Institute Photo)

WILHELM SIHLER
(Concordia Historical Institute Photo)

HENRY C. SCHWAN
(Concordia Historical Institute Photo)

WILHELM LOEHE
(Concordia Historical Institute Photo)

100

OTTOMAR FUERBRINGER
(Concordia Historical Institute Photo)

ADAM ERNST
(Concordia Historical Institute Photo)

101

JOHANN FRIEDRICH BUENGER
(Concordia Historical Institute Photo)

STEPHAN KEYL
(Concordia Historical Institute Photo)

102

F. LOCHNER
(Concordia Historical Institute Photo)

E. A. BRAUER
(Concordia Historical Institute Photo)